"In his heart and on the page, Muse contemplates the widest breadth of passions, eliding divisions too familiar in much traditional nature writing. He artfully and honestly considers place and race, wildness and domesticity, depression and elation. These essays are graceful and full of grace, pure pleasure to read."

—ANA MARIA SPAGNA, AUTHOR OF *UPLAKE*

"Muse is a ranger, and these essays range, span, and wander, considering landscape, time and identity as they go. He may be restless, childless, fatherless, but he is not rootless, and this brave book helps to root him, anchor him. As it was for the great writers who are his heroes, essaying is the means by which Muse gathers and ponders the things that make him himself. That make *us* ourselves."

—BOB COWSER JR., AUTHOR OF *GREEN FIELDS*

"Muse is my kind of writer. A wanderer, a searcher, a Southern Western Hoosier, a son of a difficult father, and a displaced man with a deep sense of place. His essays are an attempt to ground truth experience, to present life not in theory but in its messy complexity. Importantly, he follows his own advice to tree huggers—go outside!—and from his ramblings he has brought back this gift for us."

—DAVID GESSNER, AUTHOR OF *ALL THE WILD THAT REMAINS*

"Muse has given us a fantastic book—moving, humble, thought-provoking, and humorous. He admits to writing about his own wants and fears but strives for the reader to see herself. He accomplishes just that in *Dear Park Ranger* by offering exactly what he looks for in an essay: an intimate voice, an honest soul, and, most importantly, 'a wandering, wondering mind.' I was swept along with Muse's interrogation of memories and meanings."

—IRIS GRAVILLE, AUTHOR OF *HIKING NAKED*

"These essays are deeply resonant and restless, roaming over varied geographies and eras, searching inward and outward to trace Muse's roots and the threads of their impact on his marriage and identity. He mulls over the nature of change itself, writing, 'A real man, I know now, stretches.' Gorgeous sentences add up here to more than the sum of their parts, creating a whole that will linger for lucky readers."

—SONYA HUBER, AUTHOR OF *PAIN WOMAN TAKES YOUR KEYS*

"Underlying this collection of introspective essays centering on men is the respect and honor Muse bestows upon his single mother. For Muse, loving the land was the easy part of growing up. It was his mother's steadfast belief in him that gave him the strength to survive the rest, while her love fostered in him the ability to love his dear park ranger so deeply. It is a pleasure to read this quiet tribute to strong women."

—KATHRYN WILDER, AUTHOR OF *DESERT CHROME*

"In these finely crafted essays, Muse braids together two love stories—one, his love for America's wildlands, the mountains, forests, and rivers not yet devastated by human appetites; the other, his love for his wife, whose career as a park ranger carries them from place to place. With each move, Muse must reinvent himself, reconceiving his identity. Anyone who has searched for meaning in an uprooted life, weathered the storms of a long marriage, or rejoiced in untamed nature, will recognize a kindred soul."

**—SCOTT RUSSELL SANDERS,
AUTHOR OF *THE WAY OF IMAGINATION***

"In a marketplace obsessed with writers under thirty, here's a phenom over fifty. Not the fireweed flashing after the clearcut, not the ephemeral glacier lily, Muse is a sturdy cedar gnarling into aged beauty. In this wondrous book you'll come upon an old friend—honest and true, not unhurt, hopelessly in love with the land."

—TED O'CONNELL, AUTHOR OF *K: A NOVEL*

"To the great list of wondering, wandering, wide- and clear-eyed American writer/naturalists, go ahead and add the name Jeff Darren Muse. Love, loss, landscape, regret, forgiveness, and the vagaries of time—Muse reckons with it all here, in essays that make you want to hit the trail with someone you cherish."

—JOE WILKINS, AUTHOR OF *FALL BACK DOWN WHEN I DIE*

DEAR PARK RANGER

ESSAYS ON MANHOOD,
RESTLESSNESS,
AND THE GEOGRAPHY
OF HOPE

JEFF DARREN MUSE

WAYFARER BOOKS
BERKSHIRE MOUNTAINS, MASSACHUSETTS

WAYFARER BOOKS
WWW.WAYFARERBOOKS.ORG

All Rights Reserved
Published in 2023 by Wayfarer Books
Cover Design and Interior Design by Leslie M. Browning
Cover Image © Cate Bligh
Map Source: GISGeography.com
TRADE PAPERBACK 978-1-956368-52-9
EBOOK 978-1-956368-36-9

10 9 8 7 6 5 4 3 2 1

Look for our titles in paperback, ebook, and audiobook wherever books are sold.
Wholesale offerings for retailers available through Ingram.

Wayfarer Books is committed to ecological stewardship.
We greatly value the natural environment and invest in conservation.

PO Box 1601, Northampton, MA 01060

860.574.5847 | info@homeboundpublications.com

HOMEBOUNDPUBLICATIONS.COM & WAYFARERBOOKS.ORG

For Paula

CONTENTS

INTRODUCTION

GROUND TRUTHING

The pieces gathered in this book are essays, by which I mean they are experiments in making sense of things, and they are personal, by which I mean the voice speaking is the nearest I can come to my own voice.

—SCOTT RUSSELL SANDERS, *The Paradise of Bombs*

One Sunday morning when I was newly married, I so loved a woman—and life—that I crawled with my bride through soggy evergreens to trace the PVC pipe running from the spring that flowed to our kitchen, our laundry, and our bathroom, including a gurgling toilet with an icy seat. We combed the pipe for squirting, hissing, the bite marks of an up-early black bear, and the previous leaks my wife and her former housemates had taped and clamped, retaped and reclamped, because those patches would disintegrate, killing the suction. We laughed as I fumbled with the utility knife, with numb-dumb fingers and smeared eyeglasses, debating whether we needed to buy more supplies twenty miles downriver at Concrete or twice that far in Sedro-Woolley, a town originally called Bug for its mosquitoes. That's where my office was, where springtime was. But winter still gripped the upper valley. No bugs yet. No mosquitoes. And now no tap water in the rental. So we'd hiked into woods, sopping-wet woods—"like Jeremiah Johnson," I trumpeted, Robert Redford at his beard-stubble best, as if wanting to be and needing to be could align in perfect unison—and we weren't turning around, not soon, not anytime soon, not without duct-taping the snot out of something.

"Man's work," I later boasted, though my wife had been doing it for years.

In those days, Paula and I lived in Marblemount, Washington, on the western edge of North Cascades National Park. Born in Connecticut, she stood five foot ten with long black hair, slender hipped in wool uniform pants, and had worked for the National Park Service for nearly two decades, first as a wilderness ranger on Cascade Pass, up Sahale Mountain, and high atop Copper Ridge, then in the frontcountry after a climbing accident had weakened her ankles. Trained in forestry and environmental science, Paula thrilled me with her knowledge of eagles and salmon, wolves and wolverines, and fascinating old-timers like Hazel Tracy, a petite elderly lady who lived up Ranger Station Road, long after she'd been among the valley's first horse packers and dam builders. Sometimes Paula and I would visit Hazel, initially in her little yellow house, then in a nursing home in Sedro-Woolley, where I would listen to them talk affectionately of the drippy, snowcapped landscape locals called "the Upper Skagit."

I was a newcomer, to be sure, employed by North Cascades Institute, one of the park's nonprofit partners. My cubicle sat in a multiagency headquarters down the Skagit River near I-5. But home was the Upper Skagit, a glacier-carved trough through ragged mountains, among the first on the continent to catch the storms. I'm recalling the time before Paula and I built a house a few miles west in Rockport, when we rented the Dexter place along Diobsud Creek, a Skagit tributary pronounced "die-ób-sud." It rained eighty inches a year, sometimes ninety, hell, a hundred, and the clouds would slide like a slate-gray curtain across fir- and cedar-covered peaks. Imagine that. Imagine a rundown rental in a pasture with your landlord's horses, three horses grazing in every kind of weather, but mostly mist, a steady mist. A mist that fattens all the mosses, greening stumps and boulders and sagging sheds. A mist that walks back inside with you, hanging in your jacket until July. We called it milepost 109.5, the turnoff for Dexter Lane. I'd come to know Highway 20 intimately, as a suitor, a fiancé, then a husband.

The snow line would linger above us, marking the elevation where freezing began, and since our house sat at only four hundred feet, it was relatively warm at ground level, warm enough if you dressed in wool or fleece. But storms pounded the mountains nine months of the year, giving the neighborhood its character: wave after wave of serrated ridges scoured and fractured by ice. When the snow wasn't falling, the sun melted the glaciers, feeding whitewater streams like the Diobsud—frothy, raucous, timber strewn, and not far from our back door. The autumn salmon run was especially rich; the pinks darted, wiggled, splashed. In my mind's ear I can still hear the rapids, churning, turning over rocks.

To be precise, thuds, the pounding of rock to rock. Imagine that, too, the power of a stream only knee-deep but bulldozer strong. Paula and I hiked to it every evening. In the rain, holding hands.

Most of my memories start like this—with land, with waterways. I've always been this way, having loved maps before books. In the Upper Skagit, I'd unfold a topo and squiggle a finger along a dotted line. "Have you been on this trail?" I'd ask Paula. Restless, I wanted the ground truth.

My dictionary calls that "the reality of a situation as experienced firsthand rather than by report." The ground truth is the difference between sweating up a path and only reading the sign at the trailhead. I use the term to introduce this book because I've long been drawn to its meaning, due in part to my outdoor interests but mostly because I search. Throughout my life, no matter where I've lived, manhood has been a kind of topographic map. Yet it's peer pressure or social norms telling me which route to follow: Smile, Jeff, have a beer. Make babies. Make lots of money. Buy yourself a leaf blower. Hang out at parties. Lighten up. But as the years have gone by, I haven't followed a dotted line or any clear path to my fifties, and though I'm often pleased, even proud at times, on many days I can hardly bear it. In that spirit these writings are essays, as Michel de Montaigne wrote centuries ago. An *essai* is a trial or an attempt to make sense of things, including yourself. The word is also a journey—to seek out, examine, prove. But prove what to whom, I wonder, and why does it matter anyway?

I write, you'll see, to self-interrogate, to ground truth inner terrain. Or to paraphrase Joan Didion, I write to figure out what I think. "What I want and what I fear," she said.

And then there's Bill Roorbach's advice for writing essays called *personal*. Make it "a conversation," he said, about ideas, events, and shared experiences. Indeed, I write about my own life, my own wants, my own fears, but I realize that to do it well, you the reader must also see yourself. That's what I hope for whenever I sit with an essay: an intimate voice, an honest soul, and a wandering, wondering mind.

To that end, eleven years ago, I enrolled in a creative writing program when Paula and I moved to La Crosse, Wisconsin, to salvage her career as a park ranger. Our North Cascades life was over; she would sue her previous employer for discrimination. My "low-residency" program was not in La Crosse but instead Ashland, Ohio, and when I arrived for my first on-site workshop, the hills and valleys surprised me. I'd expected a flat landscape, wiped clean by ice sheets, like the Indiana cornfields I'd known growing up in the 1970s and '80s. I loved MFA work, but our breaks even more, when I'd go for long jogs through swales and woods, circling back to trot along Main Street. There, below a busy bridge, I spotted the shimmer of Town Run, a thin waterway around which Ashland had grown, the oldest buildings pressing against it. Small fish pointed upstream, their tails swaying gently, reminding me of the salmon I'd known back in Washington, reminding me of hiking in the rain.

Standing on that bridge, I thought about the Diobsud, about our journeys upstream from its mouth, when we'd hike from the Skagit toward the creek's distant sources, or runs, as some people call them. Is Town Run the start, I wondered, for a new life and a book? Is that what an essay is, a tributary to bigger waters? No doubt, since that moment, I've ground truthed to hidden origins. I've tried to be honest with myself. I've tried to make some sense, learning from it.

As for the man behind these words, expect to join me for a search—for purpose, for companionship, for a lost father, for home. We'll travel to rural Kentucky to investigate my family's roots, and hit the trail with Beat writers and hop on a hippie bus for a graduate degree. We'll float rivers, fail at hunting, and teach tree hugging to college kids. We'll spend time with Ranger Paula, both falling in love and falling apart. To be honest, the discrimination lawsuit is beside the point—the outcome, that is. Legally, I can't say much. I shouldn't divulge names or details of Paula's settlement agreement with the federal government.

But I can talk about what that time in our lives did to us, for good and bad, and how we continue to search for belonging. More urgently, I can try to understand who I was before I met Paula, and later, in Washington, then in another state, and another. I can attempt with you, in this "conversation," to figure out what's next—*where* next—and together we can help a fifty-one-year-old man navigate marriage and career and the chronic pain that comes with degenerating spinal discs. I have those too, thanks to football, thanks to genetics. I might have a surgery on the horizon as well.

For now, we live in South Carolina, in pancake-flat Charleston. There isn't a whitewater river for a half day's drive. It's the Lowcountry, a fecund soup. We ventured here for Paula's work—she's back with the National Park Service—and I'm employed by the county park system, teaching about slavery, racism, and freedom at a historic cotton plantation. Yet someday we'll leave this town, returning west, hopefully *the* West. We miss mountains and glaciers and tumbling streams. We miss hiking in the rain. We miss ourselves.

But I know our early days weren't always better. I remember October 2003. I remember a morning in windblown mist beneath bruised, low-hanging clouds. We'd wanted to survey the aftermath of record flooding in the Upper Skagit, when a rain-on-snow event had gutted culverts along Highway 20. We took a trail through lichen-draped conifers, crossing debris far from the Diobsud's shoreline. Gray silt lay in piles where high water had ebbed, leaving heaps of bark-stripped logs. Dead salmon littered the forest, their flesh bony and rank, and we slipped and skidded on maple leaves, some twice as big as our faces. As we picked up limbs and tossed aside rocks, trying to clear our beloved route, the Diobsud sounded different, its echoes rearranged.

Around that time when the foul weather came, I was grappling with emerging back pain, exacerbated by a long commute and worrying about my mother back home. She lived in Indianapolis, more than two thousand miles away, and when she shared that she'd learned of an intestinal tumor, my own stomach twisted into knots. I feared for her life, I remember, my anxiety a bitter storm, but I kept downing ibuprofen, barely sleeping, barely awake. Still, Paula and I went outside—damn the clouds, damn the rain—even as she also struggled from the turmoil of recent months. Her own mother had passed away that year, rapidly from pancreatic cancer, and now our valley was a terrible mess like the landscape of distant loved ones. I recall how little we talked at the time, married but thirteen months. Privately, I questioned our future. A sudden high water had engulfed us.

"Still here," Paula broke the silence, when finally we stood creekside. I don't recall the sound of the words, instead watching her lips release them. Her hood was up and eyes forward, the rain streaking her wire-rimmed glasses. Her cheeks were flushed, her jaw firm. She stiffly reached for my hand.

I don't remember how I responded, or what I may have thought beside the creek. Perhaps I fretted over family, my father's drinking, his early death. Dad had been gone only five years, and Paula had never met him. I'd hardly gotten to know her mother, and she barely knew mine. A map would've helped—I was lost and scared and brooding. I was thirty-four years old, deep in the woods, ground truthing.

What I do recall, nearly two decades later, are the changes around our milepost. Chaotic logjams. Uncrossable rapids. Our favorite beach on the Diobsud was gone. The creek scarcely resembled the stream we'd loved, now ravaged by a weeklong torrent, but it kept hurtling to the Skagit, and ultimately the sea. I realize today that's what Paula meant. "Still here," she said, still flowing. Manhood is much the same: the way is onward, and only onward.

JDM
Mount Pleasant, SC

WHITE MAN, FRAGILE

I imagine one of the reasons people cling to their hates
so stubbornly is because they sense, once hate is gone,
they will be forced to deal with pain.

—JAMES BALDWIN, *Notes of a Native Son*

The Cuyahoga River caught fire in Cleveland, Judy
Garland overdosed and died, the Stonewall riots
erupted, and right after that, in Community Hospital
on the east side of Indianapolis in July 1969, two weeks before
Neil Armstrong walked on the moon, I was born. The next
month, after the Manson Family committed seven murders
in Los Angeles, four hundred thousand people attended
Woodstock in rural New York. When I was three months
old, Jack Kerouac, forty-seven, the same age as Judy Garland,
died of alcoholism and liver failure. And before I turned one,
the Ohio National Guard killed four Kent State students
protesting the Vietnam War. Neil Young immortalized the
tragedy in a song: "What if you knew her / And found her
dead on the ground / How can you run when you know?"

The country was full of unrest, and changing fast, much of
it captured in news clips between *Laugh-In* and *Hee Haw*. CBS
launched the latter to replace *The Smothers Brothers Comedy*

Hour, banned for its leftist politics. Damn hippies. My early years were full of them.

Of course, I understood little of our national consciousness even in the 1970s, except sporting events like the Super Bowl because I remember playing backyard football, the cornfield behind my house a vast, insulating sea. And I remember watching television, hours and hours of television. *The Brady Bunch. Happy Days. The Six Million Dollar Man.* I remember Steve Austin, the astronaut played by Lee Majors, surviving a fiery crash and being rebuilt as a kind of cyborg, his mechanical limbs and a squinty eye creaking with synthesizer sounds whenever he saved somebody, fought a bad guy, or ran and leapt in mighty bounds. The show's first season coincided with the Watergate hearings, not to mention the Arab oil embargo. Our economy was self-destructing due to our dependency on wasting gasoline. Stagflation, experts called it—inflation up, output down, plus rising unemployment.

What's my point? Certainly not nostalgia. Something graver. I miss optimism, even if it's the false optimism of a television protagonist. I miss feeling that life should be measured on a scale greater than hope. My point is, I get it now. I get the bionic man. Austin embodied a can-do attitude, a butt kicker, a hairy-chested hero for a country that had fallen to its knees. Maybe that's all I'm saying: I miss the illusion of kicking butt.

Now in my sixth decade, living in South Carolina, three years shy of my father's age when he passed away after a colon surgery, after his drinking combined with pain meds to crash his life for good, I miss a lot these days—and optimism tops the list. I've struggled to land lucrative work here, struggled with chronic back pain, struggled every day, it seems, with the same things countless others struggle with: a career, staying healthy, a positive attitude, a plan. Yet when I look at my wealth, it's fine. My wife and I save money. We invest. And our marriage is plenty strong, albeit labored by loss. The loss of easy laughter. The loss of things to laugh about. But by most folks' standards, I rise each morning with purpose. I teach. I'm a public servant. I meet interesting people. I don't drink.

Still, something hangs over me. What is it? What looms?

Depression, I'm told. "Situational depression." So said my doctor in the bullet points of a medical summary: degenerative disc disease, laryngopharyngeal reflux, benign prostatic hyperplasia. Then there's my family history: alcoholism, high blood pressure, colon cancer.

And now tinnitus. My left ear is ringing.

It's most likely ringing because hearing loss is taking a toll. As *Harvard Health Publishing* puts it, my "brain is producing abnormal nerve signals to compensate for missing input." The result? A phantom sound. In my case, a tea kettle. It's boiling on the stove with a breathy high-pitched shriek. I don't sleep well, which creates anxiety, and anxiety feeds depression. So, along with meditation, melatonin, and a white-noise app, which I play near my head each night, I've begun to wear hearing aids. The idea is to provide more daytime "input," especially at higher frequencies, and to mask the tea kettle sound with everything I've been missing: birdsong, traffic, the refrigerator's fan, the wind, the wider world. My life has shrunk in recent years. Will bionics reenlarge it?

In any case, I had expected to eventually wear one hearing aid because my right ear is nearly deaf. Twice in my youth, first at thirteen, after nine weeks of eighth-grade swim class, then at twenty-three, after rope-swinging into the Flat Rock River while working at a YMCA camp, I developed a rancorous ear infection. Each time it led to a cholesteatoma, a fatty, noncancerous cyst that chews through soft and hard tissues. Surgeons cleaned out the pus-filled cavity, removing the destroyed remnants of the tiniest bones in my body—the hammer, anvil, and stirrup—and then stitched together my eardrum in a hollowed-out, cavernous canal. Today I shower with a silicone plug. I haven't gone swimming in decades.

So I pop in a device—in both ears, actually, because my left, "the good one," is also failing. Is this due to age? Is it noise induced? Is it from my neighbor's unrelenting leaf blowing, or his sons sitting on their dirt bikes, revving and revving? Who knows? And who knows what I've been missing? Yet what I miss most right now, as something deep inside me shrieks, is silence. I miss calm. I miss feeling carefree like the neighbor boys. If ever I needed a can-do attitude, it's now, this situation.

This all occurred to me when I came across an elementary school project from the third grade, an article I wrote for the fictitious newspaper *Indianapolis Times*, May 2, 1978, titled "Unexpected Landing!":

> The astronauts Joe H. McDonald and Scott J. Hunt were going to land on Venus when they were attacked by meteorites and put off course. They landed on Pluto. And discovered life. They brought back a creature that looks like a hog. Joe and Scott have been rewarded for this very dangerous mission. Soon more men will go to Pluto just like Joe and Scott did.

Accompanying the article was a picture I'd drawn—something "that looks like a hog"—and more, much more: my voice, my grammatical quirks (And. And.), my sense of adventure, my restlessness. Also, a situation, though no hint of depression.

It was all laid out before me, how life gets put off course, how sometimes you get attacked if only by your parents' divorce, but you have to suck it up, land on Pluto, bring back the hog. And if you're lucky, if you stay positive, you just might be rewarded. Go figure, I was eight. I was resilient. I kicked butt.

My imagination still wanders, often at dusk. I live in the coastal sprawl of Mount Pleasant, a burgeoning suburb of Charleston. After my wife's career landed us here, we bought an old house in an old development, beautiful in an earthy way. Tree-packed yards. Surprising wildness. Squirrels, owls, copperheads. As I went for a jog the other night—a power walk, goofy—I could see my neighbors in their living rooms, their screens lit up with make-believe. What's on at eight? I wondered. Nine? Then Lee Majors popped into my head, or rather his heroic character, as my slow-motion legs raced toward a golf course where I like to meander on the cart paths. My aging body began to creak, and I could hear a voice, a steely voice, the narrator-boss Oscar Goldman: "Gentlemen, we can rebuild him. We have the technology. We have the capability to make the world's first bionic man. Jeff Muse will be that man. Better than he was before. Better! Stronger! Faster!"

Is this not a cheer for midlife, for those struggling and searching? Maybe that's what this essay is, not only a reflection on coming of age, or too often coming up short, but a pep talk, a hurrah, Joe and Scott in my head, shrieking, "Forget Venus! Land on Pluto! Tough shit! Suck it up!"

Fifty-one years raced down that cart path. Make 'em count, I thought. Be a hero.

If only it were that easy.

Paula and I moved into our house several years ago, a few days before the 2016 presidential election. We'd been living in a hotel for two weeks with our elderly cat, Sonny, until the closing paperwork had cleared and a crew of Spanish-speaking painters had completed its work. The lingering fumes were so bad, so nauseating and head pounding, that our little family slept in the garage on a mattress wedged between boxes.

Each morning, Paula would leave for her office in the National Park Service headquarters on Sullivan's Island, and I would stay back to tend to Sonny, to open windows, to set up furniture. Books and tchotchkes, books and tchotchkes. I remember waking at 3:00 a.m. on Wednesday, November 9, grabbing my phone, and learning that Hillary Clinton had lost. "Fuck!" I yelled, stirring Paula, who would lay awake for hours, bleary-eyed. "Make America Great Again" would then turn from a race-baiting campaign slogan fueled by the bitterness I could feel in my own heart—whiny, emasculated, quick to blame others—to a presidency built on narcissism and gaslighting the entire country. A country full of unrest, or at least half full of stunned liberals.

I crashed. Millions did, each in our own way. But my crash had begun much earlier, in June 2015. That's when, according to my journal, my chronic back pain began. We were still living in northern Arizona, where Paula helped manage a Park Service site in the middle of a tribal reservation, and I commuted to Kanab, Utah, to work for the nonprofit friends group of Grand Staircase-Escalante National Monument, administered by the Bureau of Land Management. Mine was a grant-funded position, tenuous, loosely defined, about $33,000 a year, requiring hours and hours of driving each week, which meant sitting, interminable sitting. It was a job, though, where jobs were scarce—the sparsely populated Colorado Plateau, where sentiment about the federal government was, to put it lightly, pissed. Pissed and combative. Appealing to small-town teachers, I conceived a wandering program called Frontier Science School and started teaching *ologies*. Biology, geology, paleontology. "The study of ancient life." But even the popularity of dinosaurs couldn't guarantee my paycheck, so I began to look elsewhere.

At nearby Zion, the nation's fourth busiest national park, I became a seasonal employee, hired by the supervisory education specialist to be, in her words, the "nature center ranger," charged with leading a small facility focused on the Junior Ranger program. Based on the interview and the GS-6 federal wage of $17.26 an hour, I had the impression that I would not only help run an interpretive operation but also coach interns and volunteers, evaluate their programs, and plenty more. But by the end of my first week, I realized less, not more, would be the case. "I'm leaving," the manager said, describing a promotion she'd accepted in Las Vegas. In her place would come another woman—energetic, competitive, younger than me—to serve as the supervisor for the rest of the season.

Relax. I'm not about to turn this into a diatribe about female bosses, or millennials, or whomever you might be imagining. The woman who took the lead deserves all the kudos I can muster. She was talented, cheery, hardworking.

Driven, actually. A micromanager, but driven. And she was already on staff in her second or third season, so definitely qualified.

The truth is, *I* was not qualified. I was ill-fitted for the situation I'd gotten myself into, unprepared to shift from being led by someone older and more experienced than me to a younger person with less experience. Twenty years less! I was not ready to accept a new supervisory style, someone reluctant to delegate, or seemingly afraid to do so. I was not ready for the hour-by-hour assignments of my time, my energy, my dreams, and, yes, my resentments—my frustration with getting older yet climbing down the ladder, from earning more than $50,000 annually in my thirties, when I directed the North Cascades Environmental Learning Center, to hitting my forties as the dutiful husband, helping my wife rise as I fell through seasonal rangering and adjunct lecturing, contract work and dead ends. Life was shrinking. I was pissed.

The Zion job did help my back, though; I walked more and drove less, overnighting in the park during my workweek. Still, I'd ache in the evening after mopping the nature center's vinyl floor or leaning over to disinfect its miniature chairs and tables where we'd held art activities and the ever-popular "Dino Discovery." Imagine thirty children at your waist, or directly in your face if you're kneeling, as you're trained to do to reach their eye level, as you should do in your green wool pants, your much revered Class A uniform. Imagine a half dozen languages circling your head. Sunburned noses and grimy hands. Kids dehydrated from one-hundred-degree heat, starving for snacks, deprived of naps, brothers and sisters shoving each other, crying, pouting, pouting over the intricate, go-slow steps of creating a fake dinosaur footprint, a minuscule impression in a plaster cast. "A trace fossil," we rangers explained, "geologic evidence of ancient life, something strong and powerful that existed long ago."

"No shit," I wanted to add. I wanted to stick my own foot in the goopy mess, to cast myself rock solid, to defy extinction. Hurrah!

By the time I lay in an MRI machine in Charleston the following year, casting my forty-eight-year-old body in pale gray imagery, things had gotten worse. I was disappearing, if not extinct. I was dragging ass, depressed.

And the situation was this: a leaking and bulging spinal disc at L5-S1, soul-sucking national politics, an indifferent town with leaf blowers everywhere, no friends, a dying kitty, a relentlessly busy wife, and rejection letter after rejection letter for jobs that went to younger candidates, typically Clemson grads or College of Charleston grads who'd interned here, volunteered there, all qualified, all driven. I know because announcements would be made on Facebook, which led me to look at LinkedIn, which showed young faces, hundreds and hundreds, which reinforced my dour outlook, which, when I think about it now, logically, objectively, with proper distance, was just gaslighting self-talk: "You're crashing, old man. Mayday."

Nevertheless, meteorites. I veered off course and hit Pluto.

But I'd already been following my own advice, what I'd say to anyone complaining about unemployment: get up, get dressed, work anywhere, find the hog. I'd taken a part-time gig at Wild Birds Unlimited for ten bucks an hour, selling birdseed and bird feeders, decorative birdbaths and bird-inspired jewelry. Then I got hired by Charleston County Parks in a wandering, ranger-like role starting at $12.75. And though I'd made progress on lessening my pain with physical therapy, acupuncture, a portable TENS unit, and night after night of working out, turning my abs and glutes and spine-supporting muscles into a young man's envy, I continued to struggle. My body was stabilizing, but not my spirit. "Two master's degrees, good for nothing."

If I can pinpoint the month I bottomed out, it was January 2018. Paula's sister in Connecticut had passed away—from divorce, depression, alcoholism—and she'd been alone, estranged from us, leaving my wife to feel infinite regret. Suddenly Paula was hobbled too, and I realized how much I relied on her, emotionally as well as financially. Yet I felt powerless to rebound, paralyzed by self-absorption. I pouted. I navel-gazed. "Yes, your sister, but what about me?"

Then one day in my county park job, which required working alone from pier to playground, I stood beside my portable work table labeled "Ask a naturalist" but decided to start *moving*. I put away the bobcat at the center of my display—a "senior critterzen," I called him, a splotchy-haired taxidermied artifact that kid after kid wanted to pet—and I put away all my teaching tchotchkes: skulls and skins, an alligator's snout, seashells and shark teeth, and plastic replicas of local wildlife, including the cutest little loggerhead sea turtle whose back-right flipper I'd tangled in a grocery bag. "A reminder," I often explained, "to help protect the environment." I boxed them up, put on my work gloves, and grabbed a litter wand and five-gallon bucket. I started collecting trash half of each day. I stopped standing in place, emasculated.

I often wonder, when Paula and I moved to South Carolina, was it solely because she'd wanted a promotion closer to her elderly father in Florida, or was it due to my struggle with long-distance commuting, or sitting, whatever I was beginning to understand as life with degenerative disc disease? Or were larger forces at work?

Back in June 2015, the same month my pain started, a twenty-one-year-old White supremacist walked into Charleston's Mother Emanuel AME Church on a warm, humid Wednesday evening. He was welcomed into a close-knit Bible study group in the cool of the church's basement, and after an hour—after arguing about Scripture—he pulled out a Glock handgun and shot ten Black parishioners, telling an eleventh that she would be spared to share the story, the story of a race war his terrorism intended to start.

Nine of the churchgoers died, including Clementa C. Pinckney, a state senator and senior pastor. Paula and I, in Arizona, watched Pinckney's funeral online, including then president Barack Obama's eulogy, which ended with "Amazing Grace." Let me be clear: our nation's president *sang* "Amazing Grace." Paula and I mourned those massacred like millions did, and pondered why, in all our years of public service, we hadn't worked anywhere emphasizing the history of African Americans, let alone White supremacy. I still don't know why, really, other than to say we hadn't needed to, or wanted to, or felt responsible for doing so. Dylann Roof, Confederate flag in hand, had been our privilege not to comprehend.

But we kept watching news clips, watching and questioning, as that symbolic flag came down not only at the South Carolina Statehouse but also in Fort Sumter, a National Park Service site at the mouth of Charleston Harbor, where the Civil War began in 1861. We watched as a flat-hat-wearing ranger, a superintendent, did more than talk about history; he made it. The fort's three successive Confederate flags were headed for a Park Service museum, where they belong. That same superintendent would also hire Paula the next year, drastically changing my trajectory. Suffice to say, by the time I worked for Charleston County Parks, interpreting a stuffed bobcat everyone mistook as a coyote, I was regularly reading the national news about racism and civil rights.

As I began to pick up litter, crossing beaches, trails, and boat ramps, I realized most of the people I saw were White despite the county's population being 25.2 percent "Black or African American," a demographic defined by the US Census Bureau. It made me think of why Paula and I had talked about moving to Charleston in the first place—not solely due to her promotion, or my back pain, but also goodwill. A naïve goodwill, but sincere. Or perhaps we'd moved because President Obama had inspired in us a sense of purpose, a call to action, a reason to serve something different from what we'd always known. "Reverend Pinckney once said," Obama eulogized, "'across the South, we have a deep appreciation of history—we haven't always had a deep appreciation of each other's history.'"

Maybe curiosity is all it was. Paula and I had wanted to grow.

Strangely, the reason still eludes me, much as my depression does. I've long been a public servant, and while most of my career has been devoted to public lands, only recently have I begun to question who feels ownership of them, who claims them, and who feels unwelcome even to visit. I remember thinking that the first day I picked up litter at McLeod Plantation Historic Site, a county park property not far from downtown Charleston. I was walking alone on the site after hours, wand and bucket in hand, and because there was little to pick up, I began to read the interpretive signs:

> The McLeod House has dominated this landscape for over 150 years, but who really occupied it and defined its history? The McLeods who owned it? The troops who commandeered it during the Civil War? Or generations of African American families who lived and worked here?

> The majority of the people who lived at McLeod Plantation, the enslaved and their descendants, did not own the house. Yet they built it, grew crops to pay for it, cleaned it, and served meals in it. Their influence, obtained through sweat and skill instead of money, is evident in the house and throughout the site—if one looks carefully.

So I did look carefully—at the McLeod House, at the row of slave cabins, at a child's fingerprints in antebellum bricks. I looked at my own predicament too. My attitude. My self-talk. I tried to tell myself that it was a blessing to roam from park to park, setting up my bobcat and teaching tchotchkes, discussing turtles and gators and snakes. A blessing to watch pelicans soaring, crabs scurrying, and dolphins rising in fish-filled shallows a stone's throw from Folly Beach, which had been racially segregated, by law, until the decade I was born.

All the while, as I roamed, the stock market cranked; my investments were growing, if not my salary. I had health insurance, no kids to support, and shopped at Trader Joe's and Whole Foods. Yet I'd see litter at every turn: Chick-fil-A cups in roadside flowerbeds, grocery bags in bushes, construction debris, moldy mattresses, Styrofoam containers and plastic bottles along the tide line of every marsh. I couldn't help but look for trash. Look, dwell, complain. "Stop!" Paula pleaded. "Stop." But I'd walk the streets of our own neighborhood, Snee Farm, named for the plantation of a "founding father," and I'd see fluorescent lightbulbs on a homeowner's curb, someone expecting the long glass tubes to be cleaned up, thrown away, disappeared into the American landscape. Broken lawn equipment. Old vacuum cleaners. Torn patio umbrellas and soiled seat cushions. They'd sit there for days and days, beyond understanding, almost beyond hope.

I suppose that's part of my situation: Charleston can feel like a trash heap. There's limitless litter here, yet BMWs and Volvos, Range Rovers and Teslas, and thousands of fancy pickups, sparkling clean, brand new. And back then I was so forlorn, working alone, feeling like a failure. But my first visit to McLeod stuck with me, so I applied to be a staff member, with a male boss, my age. By the summer of 2018, I was leading walking tours nearly full time, and as awkward as it sounds to say this, interpreting slavery began to lift my spirits—researching it, teaching it, from history to culture to power. Soon I realized something else: my depression is linked to power, or the loss of power, my own. I've been losing what I've taken for granted. Health, career, marriage, and a pristine environment.

Go figure, I've been whining. At fifty-one, my butt's kicked.

Not so fast.

It's time for the 10:30 a.m. tour at McLeod Plantation Historic Site. I've got my hearing aids in with the noise filter on because the input is overwhelming: ambulance sirens, commuter traffic, jetliners, military planes and helicopters. I can literally feel the pounding of pilings for another pier, another hotel, another house built in flood-prone soil. And leaf blowers, of course. It wouldn't be Charleston without leaf blowers. Everywhere around town, I hear an incessant, full-throttle scream.

I'm also wearing a headset—a microphone attached to a small speaker strapped to my belt. The microphone reduces the throat irritation caused by acid reflux, which can afflict anyone who repeatedly and forcefully projects their voice. My larynx has become surprisingly delicate, like the disposition of some of the people I serve. What I mean is, I'm now interpreting "difficult history," mostly for White tourists, though increasingly for diverse audiences who've heard that McLeod is not your typical *Gone with the Wind* affair.

"Slavery here," I start off, paraphrasing Adam Domby, a history professor at the College of Charleston, "was the ownership of Black people. It was oppression through violence and the threat of violence in order to extract free labor."

Arms cross. Eyes look away. I've been trained to identify "white fragility," what sociologist Robin DiAngelo calls the discomfort and defensiveness displayed by White Americans whenever we talk about race. It's especially interesting to compare this to how Black or African American visitors act during a tour. They do not look away, but instead at me, or *through*, and I suspect some wonder how their interpreter, a middle-aged White man, came to talk this way. "I'm a longtime park ranger," I offer, "but new to this subject matter." In other words, awkward at times, uncomfortable, fragile. I've also become more aware. That's why, for instance, I capitalize W as well as B, realizing the social construct of race has profound implications for how one moves through the world.

"Before we walk onto the grounds," I continue, "let's keep two things in mind. First, this was not always a thirty-seven-acre historic site." Prior to the Civil War, McLeod Plantation, a slave labor camp emphasizing sea island cotton production, was fifty times larger, nearly seventeen hundred acres, making it the fifth largest of twenty-one plantations on James Island. "According to the US census in 1860, the population of this island included roughly two hundred White people, all free, and more than fifteen hundred Black people, all enslaved. Or to put it another way, 13 percent enslaved 87 percent. How was that possible?"

Racism, I explain, with legal authority and institutional control. "Your gut is telling you how it happened: hired guns on slave patrols, whippings, salt put in the wounds, malnutrition, outlawing reading and writing, and the constant threat of sexual assault, family separation, and being sold off, never to return."

But enslaved people resisted. They slowed down the work, feigned illness, stole food, and poisoned it. They sabotaged the cotton gin. They created religion and music and a creole language. They murdered. They ran. They kept their heads down, trying to survive. "We cannot comprehend this history," I say, "without understanding the intensity and urgency of daily life here. Our forebears, both Black and White, pioneered Charleston's race relations."

Then I note the second thing: "People called McLeod Plantation home until 1990. White people as well as Black." Arms recross. Faces frown. Many White visitors, I have learned, are uncomfortable not only talking about race, but also being identified as White. DiAngelo calls it "race-based stress" due to an expectation of "racial comfort" in a predominantly White nation.

"The final White man to live here was Willie McLeod, the grandson of the slave owner." Willie was born in 1885 and died in 1990. He never met his grandfather, a Confederate soldier who owned seventy-four to one hundred human beings and whose wealth was valued at $105,000 in 1860, or more than three million dollars today. "Willie was never married and never had any children. When he died, he willed this site to the Historic Charleston Foundation, which eventually sold it to my employer, Charleston County Parks." The county bought the property for $3.3 million in 2011 and completed four years of restoration while gathering community feedback to conceive an interpretive theme: "'Transition to Freedom,' a reminder that the majority of people who lived here, all the way to 1990, were Black. They descended from ancestors in Africa, the Caribbean, and throughout the Southeast Coast."

In McLeod Plantation's latter years, several people had no choice but to rent the former slave cabins, paying the elderly man they called "Mister Willie," and then facing eviction upon his death. But their lives, and the lives of their ancestors, reveal a broad span of history, from generations of bondage, to the Civil War, to Reconstruction and Jim Crow, to the Civil Rights Movement and beyond. "As we consider enslaved people and their descendants, if we expect to learn from them, we must talk about not only the oppression they faced, but also the qualities they demonstrated while resisting oppression. Strength. Resilience. And definitely courage." That's what I keep sensing every time I step onto this site: a profound courage on the part of African Americans to move forward no matter the circumstances. "You're missing out unless you learn this. We all need to learn this."

That last line is about as close as I can get to understanding how I ended up at McLeod. Did Obama send me? Did Donald Trump, who in 2017, after a deadly White supremacists' rally in Charlottesville, Virginia, called many of those participants "very fine people"?

Sure, both presidents played a part. But the person who keeps me coming back is a young girl named Leia, who was born into slavery in the 1850s and passed away in 1933. She walked onto McLeod Plantation at four to seven years old, near the start of the Civil War, and arrived alone, having been sold and separated from her parents at an auction house downtown.

"How do we know about Leia?" I ask, as we step in and out of buildings. We know she existed because of oral history—her family's history, which includes the Browns, the Robinsons, the Richardsons, and other local people, predominantly African Americans. And we know she existed because the 1860 census for this plantation, specifically a tax document called a slave schedule, records the presence of female children. "She may be nameless in this document, but she's here, or she arrives soon after, living alongside more than seventy moms and dads, sons and daughters—chattel slaves owned by William Wallace McLeod."

Standing beneath sprawling live oaks, we talk about one of Leia's earliest memories, which she passed on to family members such as her granddaughter, Edna "Mattie" Richardson. Edna was born on McLeod Plantation in 1914, during Jim Crow segregation and tenant farming, and lived locally until her death in 2012. We interpreters try to work with her descendants to get the narrative right. Our tours involve primary sources of information, family photos, maps, and interviews.

Edna, in an interview with Eugene Frazier Sr., a local African American historian, said that when she was a little girl, her grandmother, Leia, shared details from a forced march, which also included Leia's parents. The group walked dozens of miles, presumably in shackles. Slave traders called that a *coffle*, from an Arabic word meaning "caravan."

I bring Leia to life:

Leia remembered, Edna said, that the adults in her group were blindfolded as they traveled during daylight hours. They walked through a forest on a sandy path, and at times through creeks and swamps. She remembered getting into a boat to cross a body of water, not the ocean but a short trip crossing a big river or Charleston Harbor. Their feet were bruised and bloody, Leia remembered, as they walked on cobblestone streets, and when they entered a small building downtown, they were given rags and newspapers to wipe themselves off, to clean up, to prepare. What kind of building had she entered?

"A slave market," my audience responds. I've made eye contact with each of them.

The stories go on and on, at least they could, but my tour should last only an hour, then it's time for conversation or letting visitors amble alone, reflecting on what they have learned or felt or what they can't easily accept as our nation's history. For instance, a recent online reviewer, anonymous, called me "the biggest snowflake tour guide I've ever heard," reminding me that the Trump era will forever be remembered for name calling. Yet others, like Krishin Parikh, give me hope, a hope that what I'm doing now suits my career as well as the times: "Jeff was an incredibly smart and engaging tour guide. I truly felt like I was walking on that soil in the nineteenth century."

Most visitors keep walking, toward Wappoo Creek, now the Intracoastal Waterway, riprapped and dredged. Along its wooded bank lies an African American cemetery with more than one hundred graves, a few marked with headstones. According to archaeologists, the sites date from the mid-1700s to the mid-1900s, and buried with many are seashells, "vessels" symbolizing water, a means for the spirit to cross over into the next life. I often wonder where Leia was laid to rest, if she too made the journey. She had the courage, the grit, which inspires me to no end.

A week after my tenth birthday, in July 1979, President Jimmy Carter delivered his prime-time address, "A Crisis in Confidence," perhaps the most courageous political speech I've ever read. I actually did watch the address, a portion of it. Or rather, I remember hearing Carter's voice, a soft-spoken, melodic voice, part preacher, part professor:

> I ask Congress to give me authority for mandatory conservation and for standby gasoline rationing. To further conserve energy, I'm proposing tonight an extra ten billion dollars over the next decade to strengthen our public transportation systems. And I'm asking you for your good and for your Nation's security to take no unnecessary trips, to use carpools or public transportation whenever you can, to park your car one extra day per week, to obey the speed limit, and to set your thermostats to save fuel. Every act of energy conservation like this is more than just common sense—I tell you it is an act of patriotism.

President Carter, I'd later understand, was addressing America's energy crisis, which had compounded the nation's economic woes and contributed to a loss of confidence in the federal government. But Americans, I'd also learn, aren't Carter's kind of patriot. We're fragile conservationists. We prefer hardliners, not hard truths.

I bring up the speech not only because I find it remarkable that a US president asked We the People to do without, but also because of Carter's accent. The fact is, as a kid, I didn't trust Carter for the simple reason that he was a southerner. And White southerners, I knew—I thought I knew, anyway—had been responsible for racism. That is, like 140 million other Americans in January 1977, I'd watched all eight episodes of *Roots*, based on Alex Haley's novel about his fourth-great-grandfather, Kunta Kinte, and all who had descended from him. I'd seen Kunta shackled in the bowels of a slave ship and rebelling with other Africans, and I'd felt both fear and pleasure when he sunk a knife into Ralph Waite's gut. You remember Ralph Waite, who played John-Boy's dad on *The Waltons?* Lo, he was murderous! A nasty White man on Kunta's slave ship. Devastated, I couldn't stomach *The Waltons* after that.

But here's the thing: Kunta was played by two actors, LeVar Burton when Kunta was young and John Amos when he was older. Both would be lauded for their roles. Until the miniseries *Roots*, which aired nightly on ABC for more than a week, I hadn't been exposed to Black history. I doubt I'd met a single African American up to that point. As I recall, none were attending my elementary school in Mt. Comfort, Indiana, and perhaps none lived in my entire county, rural Hancock County, about an hour's drive from Marion, where the Hoosier State's last lynching occurred in 1930.

Yet I had known Amos from *Good Times,* a half-hour sitcom about a Black working-class family in urban Chicago, and

I distinctly remember that his character, James Evans, had already mesmerized me with his powerful, resonant voice; his thick shoulders in a long-sleeved flannel shirt; the way his balding brow exuded emotion whenever he disciplined his kids or hugged his wife; and how he was constantly grinding, adapting, in whatever way he had to, as a father, as a man. He embodied the struggle against "racial and economic discrimination," as Robin R. Means Coleman wrote in *African American Viewers and the Black Situation Comedy.*

James's wife, three children, and a wide-ranging cast rounded out the show's personalities, but only as an adult would I understand why Amos had left *Good Times* after its third season, the height of its popularity. He disagreed with the writers—White writers—on the increasing buffoonery of the character JJ, James's oldest son, played by Jimmie Walker. Everyone remembers JJ, who called himself Kid Dyn-O-Mite! "With a focus on [JJ's] schemes and lawless antics," Coleman wrote, "punctuated by blackvoice and attire that seemed to come straight from Sambo's closet, this series lost any glimmer of Black subjectivity." And I get that now. I get how, as a little boy, a White boy with a single mother, I admired James, the stalwart father, while giggling at JJ, the buffoon—what Amos would call degradation, playing on racist stereotypes forged by White minstrels in blackface. Was I learning to be a bigot? Is it outlandish to say that?

Nonetheless, had Amos not left *Good Times,* he might not have been in *Roots,* and had he not been in *Roots,* I might not have watched every scene, from a centuries-old Gambian village, to a slave ship, to a plantation, to resistance and war and the stony road to freedom. I wouldn't have watched Kunta Kinte, a runaway—a self-emancipating Black man enslaved by White people—get caught by pattyrollers, who then severed his foot.

Yet he survived. The Black man survived. Strength, resilience, courage. I began to understand, thanks to Amos.

What's my point? Certainly not nostalgia. Something graver. Something far more significant that I hadn't grasped until now. What I'm saying is, my first childhood hero wasn't "Steve Austin, astronaut. A man barely alive." It wasn't Lee Majors in *The Six Million Dollar Man*. It was James Evans, and Kunta Kinte, and the actor John Amos. My first hero was Black. And my situation today, in Charleston—a town filled with plantations that conceived and nurtured White supremacy, that helped build a nation that couldn't do without, and wouldn't dare—might make perfect sense. I've landed at McLeod Plantation Historic Site because it's one of the spots Dylann Roof visited before murdering nine people. Moms and dads, sons and daughters. Indeed, during my interpretive tours, I sometimes share a laminated image, a selfie Roof took in front of the McLeod House two months before committing the massacre. "What's he thinking?" I ask, holding his portrait near my chest. Hatred, visitors know. Roof scowls in the photo, inspired.

As for my own inspiration, it's a cruel one. I can't say that I'm comfortable, let alone optimistic. The self-loathing is always there—a low wage, no benefits. And sometimes I feel it from coworkers, a disdain for who I am. A young Black woman shuns me. "You're a White man," my boss said. Of course, I ponder everyone's privilege, every day come lunchtime, as our office smells of fast food and so much waste goes unrecycled. I know I can't control these things, including Sonny, our cat. He passed away after nineteen years, and Paula has yet to recover. And now my ears have gone haywire, though hearing aids help. I pop them in and put on my headset, wading into the wider world. I *chose* this path, I tell myself. Suck it up. Rebuild.

I REMEMBER THE DOGS

In the snapshot I'm five years old, my skin tan, a little belly, and I'm frowning in pain. Behind me sits Dad's Chevy, a metallic silver Impala.

It's June 1975 in central Indiana. My skull is wrapped in a swirl of bandages, my hair unwashed, nearly blond. My sullen eyes look straight at the camera, toward whom I can't recall. But I remember posing for that portrait beside a hazy, half-grown cornfield, where my parents had built a brick one-story next to Mom's mother, Grandma, and her quiet second husband. Though he wasn't in the photo with me, my brother, Alan, stood nearby, his blood-soaked dressings from a shoulder wound oozing beneath a T-shirt. Twelve years old with coke-bottle eyeglasses and already a muscular chest, he was "built like a Burkhart," Mom once said, referring to Buck, whom Grandma had married first. I was tiny—three and a half feet tall, forty-five pounds or so—but in bandages I looked like a war vet just home from Vietnam. Sixteen stitches laced my head, sealing a jagged five-inch gash. Two more on my nose. Six through my left eyebrow. The black threads dangled in my peripheral vision, stinging and swollen, and I dabbed at the ones in my crusty nostril as if I'd broken my face. I'd never felt hurt like that. It's my first memory of hurt.

The sutures were sewn down south, where Alan and I had wrecked a minibike into a barbed wire fence. "An accident," everyone kept saying, though I sensed unspoken blame. A few weeks earlier, Dad had given it to my brother as a gift for growing up, the way blue-collar men doted on their sons in driveways throughout the Midwest. He'd bought it used from a coworker at Chrysler, a whim perhaps, a good deal. I thought it was beautiful, a big toy but tough. I loved its knobby tires, its chrome muffler that looked like a machine gun, and when I see the color burgundy today, I still think of that minibike's gas tank. It was Alan's, I knew, but I celebrated all the same, and the weeknight Dad came home with it, I begged and begged for a ride.

"No," Mom said. "You're too small. Stay off it."

What if I had listened to her? What would I remember then?

Two days before the scene in the photograph, Dad took Alan and me to visit his maternal grandparents near Glasgow, Kentucky, a four-hour drive down I-65 past the turnoff for Mammoth Cave. We called them Mama and Papa Shaw, a surname that came from Scotland, though the British Isles were a world away in picture books and TV shows. Mama made biscuits and gravy for breakfast, took slop out back to the hogs, and loved to carry on with Dad as he pulled beers from a Styrofoam cooler. Papa Shaw was in his eighties, which made him the oldest person we knew. In a faded John Deere ball cap, he mumbled contentedly to himself. He'd lean over his red leather armchair to spit tobacco into a brass can, peppering the floor with misses—a sticky minefield on vinyl tiles. My shoes felt gluey and slow whenever he pulled me in close, and my eyes would settle on the glistening slurry in the depths of his sour spittoon. Fear, fascination, hesitant hugs. A great-grandkid's kind of love.

Not long after we arrived on a Friday, Dad pulled out the minibike from the Impala's massive trunk. Maybe it would help his eldest son endure a friendless weekend. Mom had stayed behind in Indiana, nursing a staph infection, though even then, I'd later learn, their marriage was nearing its end. On Saturday morning, Alan rode along Cherokee Trail Road, a gravel lane angling off the highway near Mama and Papa's front yard. I remember standing by the mailbox, shirtless in sunshine. I wore royal blue cotton shorts. No belt. No shoes. And I must've wondered where my big brother went whenever he sped away. From that spot I could also see Dad talking with Mama in the carport. He sat on the swing, smoking a cigarette and holding an aluminum can. My father always smoked and drank. Back then I thought nothing of it.

At the time no one knew that Alan was teasing two dogs at the end of the dead-end lane, what any kid might do, thoughtless of the repercussions. Each trip he stopped in front of a neighbor's house, cranking the throttle in neutral, until the animals came running, furious at the noise. I couldn't hear the commotion, a half mile distant; all I saw was Alan return, smiling, even laughing. So when he slid back on his seat, offering a ride, I didn't think about Mom—or shoes, a shirt, a helmet. Instead, climbing onto the burgundy gas tank, I felt its heat spread along my thighs, felt the whine of the engine beneath me, and felt my eyes tear up in the wind. I remember zipping down the road, the ground blurring beneath my tanned feet. I remember revving at the turnaround, riling up those farmhouse dogs.

When Alan popped the clutch, the fenders clanged and banged, and the minibike crouched like a wild creature as the tires dug into the gravel. A fierce sensation clawed through me—barks and snarls alongside our legs. Teeth gnashed near our kneecaps. The dogs' hair stood on end. My heart seized as I squeezed the bar between Alan's arms and white-knuckled hands, and I felt his right leg twitch as he clicked through a series of gears. We blazed down the road in a dust cloud of ricochet sounds, my fright giving way to a thrilling rush, the elation of escape.

That minibike was fast. Those dogs never had a chance.

Perhaps a memory of the wreck lies somewhere deep inside me, the twists of metal first tearing through my hair and then nearly a hazel green eyeball. Or maybe from the other direction as I tumbled or flew: left nostril, left eyebrow, the left side of my skull. In that order, gouged.

What I do recall is standing up, shell-shocked, the sharp rocks like broken glass beneath my shoeless feet. My chest heaved with sobs. My head stung and spun. Everything was red and blurry. The minibike ticked as its engine cooled, muffler side up in the ditch. Black cows lingered like shadows, tails swinging, undisturbed. Their mouths gnawed at the silvery grass flattened by the wreck. The barbed wire held them back as I hobbled through blood spatter, the gravel feeling like a thousand slivers cutting me with every step.

My brother didn't black out; adrenaline had masked the moment when the barbed wire raked his shoulder. We'd shot off the road after hitting a pothole, the dogs trailing close behind. Stunned by my screaming, he watched me leak—like a Ball jar, cracked—the blood streaming down my legs into dust slightly less red. Then he picked me up, running back to the dog owner's farmhouse. What did she think, I wonder, and how did we get past her animals? When I asked Alan about it recently, he said, "The dogs didn't even bark."

For me, what remains of the wreck are snippets from the hours that followed. A stranger's towel on my face, wiping, wiping, wiping. An echo in Mama and Papa's house— someone's on the phone, yelling. And I remember lying on Uncle Stanley's lap in the front seat of the Chevy Impala. My legs pressed into my father's thighs as I writhed back and forth in pain, and as we sped to the hospital in Glasgow, Stanley pressed firmly against my head. Pulling my hair aside to expose my scalp, he spoke with a deep Kentucky drawl. "Keith," he said to his big brother, "here's what's bleeding so much."

I also remember Dad's face: he's crying, hands on the wheel. Crying and swearing. Glassy eyes. Bloodshot. "I never should've bought that fucking minibike!" A curse word, percussive. I hear it again as I lie beneath a light getting stitches. Twenty-four in all. Needles, tweezers, scissors.

I wish I could recall pulling into our drive in Indianapolis the next day. Dad had traveled from his birthplace dozens and dozens of times. But how did he feel on this trip north with two silent sons in tow, and what did Mom feel when the Impala's doors swung open? I imagine her in shorts and a halter-top walking out to meet us, her jaw rigid with adult emotions, her own eyes glassy with fear. Was she furious or heartbroken at the sight of us? Did Dad hang his head with guilt? Did his breath smell like alcohol, or was he sober for this reunion? All I know is what I see in the photograph, how I'm standing in front of the Impala. My expression conveys not only discomfort, but also sadness, maybe shame. I'm wearing a button-up shirt with blue pinstripes over a bright white tee. I'm all dressed up at the height of summer, the first grade still weeks away.

Human lives can read like reckless stories, damaged and tragic, and the mind often lies beyond our control—some thoughts and feelings we hold onto, others disappear. But looking at that photo of myself next to my father's silver Chevy, I'm transported back into bandages, into stitches, into confusion. It's a four-decade-old snapshot, a hurtful moment, a half memory, but even now, sliding a finger through my hair, I feel the ridge of scar tissue. Whenever I cut my hair short, anyone can see it, and whenever someone asks about it, I look for their scars in turn.

Still, I can't help but see a little boy wrestling with blame. He not only wrecked his face, he thought, but also his parents' marriage. My mother says divorce was inevitable—Dad drank and chased women—and that I was only a child, Alan not even a teenager. But coincidence seems unlikely because I remember my birthday that July. Dad handed me a gift, a small box wrapped imperfectly. I pulled out a green sweatshirt with a red "6" across the chest. Dad said it matched my age, that I was getting big, growing up. Was it then, sitting on the edge of my bed, he told me he was moving out? I may not have understood why at the time, but I'm sure I felt responsible.

Indeed, as I write this, I'm twice the age of my father at the time of the minibike wreck, and I tend to think one weekend reveals everything that a family is, if not all that it will become. My mother would go on to remarry and divorce a second time, for decades living near Grandma, who, alongside her third husband, would lose much of her memory. Mom put two kids through college and started a successful business, and never have I heard her second-guess a decision regarding the men in her life. My brother also divorced, got remarried, has three kids, and often hovers fretfully, which for years he directed at me. When our father died in 1998, due in part to his lifelong drinking, I think Alan felt an awkward relief that Keith Muse would no longer stop by. It's different for my brother. He remembers more than I do.

As for me, I have no children, though I've been married for two decades. Paula and I often look at photographs, telling stories to make sense of things. If we did have kids, I wonder, would we worry every moment? I'm sure we'd never buy a minibike, but there'd always be something, right? Sports, roughhousing, a moment's distraction, a weakness like Dad's addiction. How does any childhood go unscathed, or any family unburdened? I may not be a parent myself, but I can understand one's regret.

Scientists say the universe was born some thirteen billion years ago, the big bang theory their best explanation for the origin of everything. Before then, the theory suggests, all matter was infinitely dense, bound together in a single whole, unstable, immeasurably hot. No time or space existed, then suddenly both did.

That weekend was my own big bang, or maybe the weeks surrounding it, because try as I might, I can't remember our lives before the spring of 1975. Sure, there are earlier photographs, the four of us huddling together. I'm smiling. My brother's smiling. Mom and Dad are too. Yet it's someone else's life, beyond memory, beyond comprehension. I can't conceive of us together, like the universe before existence.

What should I make of all this—what's missing and what remains? My first memories are of Dad's drinking, his drowning eyes, "that fucking minibike." And what about Mom, or how she felt when the car doors opened? Though I can't remember it, I've watched her for decades since. Men have failed her too often, even her own dad, Buck.

Then there's my big brother, Alan, whose scars look worse than my own. The barbed wire sliced through his knuckles and furrowed his muscular shoulder. Everyone was so worried about me they neglected to take him to the hospital. Instead, Mama Shaw scrubbed his wounds, and scrubbed and scrubbed some more. I imagine him enduring her vein-laced hands, the coarse washrag, and scalding bathwater, his guilt rising as sure as blood, expanding to its own sort of galaxy.

Then again, I'm the one who begged and begged for a ride. Maybe what happened is my fault: a kid can steer his whole family. I remember gripping the handlebars. I remember the dogs.

AN ARK OF THE HEART

I have a metaphor. I say, "Look, you're in a car, your new selves can get in, but your old selves can't get out." You can bring new vision and guidance into your life, but you can't lose or forget who you've been or what you've seen. New people can get in, but nobody ever gets out: The child from 1950, he doesn't get out. The teenager, the adolescent boy, no one can get out. They are with you until the end of the ride, and you're going to pass a certain amount of them on. The key is, of course, who's driving.

—BRUCE SPRINGSTEEN,

Rolling Stone interview, March 29, 2012

I was a college sophomore when I fell for Mia, an athletic blonde from the Pacific Northwest, a junior. Iridescent green eyes. Full lips. A tongue that tasted of alcohol. Kissing her warmed my mouth like a faint chemical burn, like the halo of a small flame. I remember how it felt because I didn't drink. Not beer. Not vodka. Not Mad Dog. Nothing my fraternity brothers poured at Sigma Alpha Epsilon, SAE for short.

Mia, however, enjoyed our parties, a red cup in her hand like the dozens of other sorority girls who packed the dance floor outside my room, which was located in the basement close to the bar. She was the first woman I ever kissed who had liquor on her breath, though I can't recall how I met her, perhaps after one of her volleyball matches when I caught her eye and said, "Good game." Or on the way to class one morning, feeling bold, I said hello. Either way, chance, a fluke, dumb luck.

And how did I end up living in that basement, an experience like no other? As I recall, fraternity brothers chose their rooms based on seniority, grade point average, and, I figured, pot smoking kept under wraps. I may have been the only nondrinker in the house, sixty guys from mostly well-to-do families, the cockiest from New Canaan, Connecticut, and Chicago suburbs like Glencoe—money, everyone knew. That fall, I'd landed at the bottom of the stairs, where beer kegs were dragged like sandbags in the afternoon and tossed like tin cans hours later. I remember now, after our parties, after most people had gone home and I lay in bed, trying to sleep, the cheers of drunken young pledges forced to leap rolling kegs. Donkey Kong, they called it. Jump, frat boy! Jump!

When people ask why I lived in a fraternity, I grasp for a reason. I'm grasping now. How do you make sense of it—an alcoholic's son amid all the booze? In 1987, the year I entered DePauw University, more than three quarters of its freshmen pledged a fraternity, and like most, I wanted to belong, to be popular, to be a stud. We moved in the week before classes got started, a practice the school has since changed. Imagine a honeymoon phase of virile popularity, when I paraded like a stallion through "rush week." I was arrogant like everyone else, though chosen from SAE's "second list." Even so, I shook hands and toured its parent-free mansion, intrigued by the promise of status. An elegant living room led to the echoes of a dining hall. Huge stereos pounded in bedrooms. And I saw elaborate, custom-built lofts in those bedrooms, queen mattresses beneath poster-covered ceilings. I pictured all the girls climbing toward those beds, their tanned legs achingly beautiful.

College was craving, I see now. Craving and fitting in.

I also see books had yet to enter my thoughts and that I fretted until SAE chose me. I kept fretting, of course, after I got in, especially through long, rowdy weekends. Good thing I met Mia the next autumn; better still, she dropped out. Had she not invited me out west for a visit, I might've started drinking. I might have.

In his 1957 novel, *On the Road*, Jack Kerouac penned one of my favorite passages: "Beyond the glittering street was darkness and beyond the darkness the West. I had to go."

At times I've said that's how *I* started, that I read Kerouac's words and stepped toward the mountains, toward the man I would one day become. I've said I was hungry for wide-open spaces and experiences I couldn't find in Indiana. In truth, I credit Mia's forlorn letters, which I'd read before anything by

Beat writers, her postmark from Astoria, Oregon, thousands of miles distant, like a dream.

What I mean is, this was before texting and email. Before googling images of a place or reading about it online. Before the World Wide Web, I suppose. What I knew of the origin of that postmark was little more than an encyclopedia entry in DePauw's library. All I had were Mia's stories of growing up in Washington, and her letters from Oregon. Actually, cards, probably a Valentine's Day card, packed with sadness and yearning and vivid lines about fir trees and Victorian houses and her mother's tiny art gallery near a pier on the Columbia River, a few miles from the stormy Pacific. I can't remember the gallery's name, but I have something from it: a salmon. Or rather I have an artist's imagining of a salmon, a conjuring of scrap metal and recycled wood, old nails and speckles of gray and gold paint that create the impression of fish scales. It's primitive, earthy, beautiful. It's two feet long and still on my wall, mere inches from this keyboard. And it occurs to me now that long-ago gift is the earliest, most tangible reminder of why I first headed west, or anywhere, why I've followed this path, searching, searching, searching, not only as a way of life but as the foundation of my identity: a girl. There is always a girl.

It was late March 1989. Mia had left DePauw three months earlier to live with her mom and stepdad in Oregon, and since she'd dropped out to earn money for tuition, I scrounged up enough for the airfare. I flew to Portland on a Friday afternoon, though the sun had already set before my arrival, and Mia had previously warned me of the rain, how soggy the place was, how dank. But as the jet glided down toward the runway, I could see a hulking darkness below—the storied Columbia I'd admired on a map, the route for Indigenous people and White explorers. And as we drove downriver to Astoria, one of the oldest settlements on the West Coast, Mia described the town's founding in 1811, six years after Lewis and Clark had wintered there.

I'm sure we talked about the road trip we had planned, a thousand miles to Los Angeles, then back. I'm sure we talked about missing each other. We may have even talked about the future. But what sticks with me now, decades later, is what I saw the next morning at sunrise: a cascading view across dozens of rooftops, a miles-wide river filled with boats. I counted eight enormous, orange-hulled container ships, six pointing upstream, two down. Their decks brimmed with multicolored boxes. Exotic names told of faraway lands. Streamers of gray clouds trailed across green and blue ridges—the foothills of southwest Washington—and white gulls spiraled above a latticework of piers in slow circles of undulating flight. For a Hoosier raised amid cornfields, a monotonous farmscape, landlocked, I was awestruck not only by the scenery but by what Lewis and Clark must've thought: *here.* Here is where the continent ends.

"Different, eh?" Mia may have asked, sitting in the kitchen that morning. I'd been marveling at the view for more than an hour, since waking in her bedroom upstairs. I drank French press coffee and ate a whole grain bagel—another new experience, new tastes—and I lingered with her parents, who talked about their lives on the drenched, ragged edge of America.

I have no recollection of what else we discussed. But all the ground we covered? Definitely. We started by descending to a maritime museum and walking on the deck of a historic lightship. On Sunday, Mia's mom took us back to Portland to pick up a rental car, a Ford Taurus, then her daughter and I sped south through the Willamette Valley, hoping for San Francisco overnight. Soon after we crossed into California, I awoke in the passenger seat. An ethereal golden light flooded the car, and I sat up to peer out the windshield. Mount Shasta loomed at sunset—snowbound, radiating. Mia smiled silently, her blonde curls sparkling, as I struggled to make sense with my eyes.

I understand now I had never seen alpenglow, let alone a glacier-clad volcano. I was mesmerized by the light, the beauty of a girl, and how meltwater gathered into threads. How high is that summit? I wondered. How long till its streams reach the sea? We rounded the mountain's mammoth shoulder. The sky turned orange, crimson, then pale blue.

As an Indiana child in the 1970s, I studied a Rand McNally atlas in the back seat, though instead of a volcano beyond the window, I saw silo-studded stretches, flat and featureless.

I remember thumbing through that atlas, asking questions about its symbols and squiggly lines. I remember the emerald shade across swaths of empty space—public land in parks and forests. Why some pages had more green fascinated me. Indiana had far less than the other states. I pondered the mystery with a finger on the Rockies, the Redwoods, the Smokies, and Yellowstone.

On trips to Kentucky, my father's birthplace, I matched the terrain beyond the window with my map, especially the blue markings I had come to understand as lakes and creeks and rivers. I recall pinpointing the Ohio—ground truthing, like a surveyor—as letters on the sign atop the bridge looked the same as those spread across my lap. Crossing into Louisville was exhilarating. Waves rolled downstream to my right. My imagination took the leap, floating along, and that big river took hold of a little kid.

Writer Stephen Trimble talks about this phenomenon in *The Geography of Childhood: Why Children Need Wild Places.* "We have map-making genes strung along our DNA," essential for the survival of our species. Recognizing landmarks, he explains, is partly how our brains develop. The process begins when we're only four or five, old enough to remember the way home. Was I piecing together North America then? Did that bridge inspire future journeys? Did I use it as a symbolic thumbtack, stringing a line outward and beyond? What I know for sure about those early trips is experiencing an age-old rite of passage. I learned how to read the language of landscapes long before reading most sentences.

Years later, traveling down the Pacific Coast, I felt the same sensation, the same desire. The same combination of wonder and excitement. A restless curiosity. Longing. Driving into San Francisco felt like Louisville—the sudden shadows of skyscrapers—and Big Sur was riven like southern Kentucky, its leafy hollows beckoning no matter how small.

Again, though, there's another truth to these memories, more to traveling with my parents as a boy. My mother and father split up when I was six and finalized their divorce two years later. The recollections I have of sitting in the backseat are far fewer than those up front, when Alan might let me ride shotgun next to whoever climbed behind the wheel. In particular, I recall trips with Dad, summers mostly, when school was out, when just the two of us would travel from central Indiana to Kentucky's Cumberland Plateau. And as we drove, I could see a can or bottle between his legs, or hear a paper bag crinkle as he lifted it. I don't recall worrying about it as a kid, though his addiction would become another journey. By the time I entered college a decade later, I would see my father occasionally and reluctantly, yet fraternity life offered constant reminders amid bloodshot eyes and sour breath. Oddly, it was comforting at times, the way the frat house smelled of cigarettes and alcohol, and kissing Mia when she was buzzed—her ease, her warmth—had a way of making me feel close to him.

Like I said, I'm grasping to make sense of this—loving people, fearing them, or both. Let's just call it what it is: attraction one minute, repulsion the next. Maybe that's why I like road trips. Movement in any direction is a relief. Or maybe I like the road because my father did. He pointed out rivers, and I leapt.

I should also admit I've tried drinking a time or two, including a kegger during my junior year in high school. It was early November between playoff games, when scores of kids had gathered in a harvested cornfield. That time of year, Indiana nights are chilly, though not winter-coat weather, with little rain. I wore a hooded sweatshirt under a black nylon jacket with a football patch sewn across the chest. The party took place at a schoolmate's trailer, about a quarter mile off a two-lane highway, and I sipped a beer while eying Josie Slater, a sultry senior who gazed right back. But as fate would have it, I didn't talk to her. Flashing lights began crowding the horizon. Next came the shouts of panicking teenagers as police cars turned into the driveway.

I'm not sure what pushed me to run; no one grabbed my arm to pull me away. Mike and Nate, the buddies I rode with, were nowhere in sight. They could lie to their parents. They'd survive. But in that moment I thought of my mother, who was camping with her second husband that weekend. What would she think if I got arrested? Would my drinking be more than she could bear?

So I bolted into the void beyond the yard, stumbling through dirt clods and corn stubble. Lying on my stomach beneath the sweep of a flashlight, I heard girls crying, a police radio, my own breath.

"Who's that?" someone said, lying near me. I didn't recognize his voice but smelled pot.

"Jeff Muse," I whispered, shivering. Giggles came from farther back in the dark.

"Muse!" the voice said. "That's hilarious. I didn't expect to see *you* running from the cops." I felt flattered and offended, my heart pounding with dread, my head swimming from the regret of a single cup.

As I write these words, I've got my yearbook open, trying to match a face to that cheerful voice, but like the darkness enveloping us in that cornfield, all I'm left with is a pot smoker's apt question. Before long, we moved beyond the trailer, slinking to a tree line near a county road. "Come with us," the voice said. "I'll give you a ride home. Hell, stay at my house if you want."

On one hand, I was inspired by the offer—a stoner and a jock teaming up—but on the other I thought of disappointing my mother. I thought of marijuana, drugs, the cops.

"Thanks, man," I said, trying to act grateful, like I wasn't scared, scared of him. "I can walk from here. It's not that far—400 West, 600 North, 500 West."

I tried to make a long slog through the night seem like nothing, nothing anyone except Mike and Nate might hear about. Yet the following spring this yearbook would be published, including a trivia game called "Student Life." Here, along the margin, are the words: "Name the junior who ran home nine miles from a party." It's easy to laugh now, to poke fun at myself, but that night, in that cornfield, I was terrified.

My mother didn't hear about that incident until she returned home with my stepdad on Sunday evening, although Alan, who was twenty-two and living with us at the time, had already scolded me like the father he had become. Worse, Mom didn't punish me for my poor judgment. Instead, she talked of choices, her voice cracking. "Jeffrey," she asked, "can I trust you?" I'd given her my car keys. She handed them back.

What remains from that walk is a memory map, a slideshow of insecurity and adventure, how I zigzagged through cornfields and barking dogs, down one county road to the lonely next. By the time I returned to school, word had spread—the party, the cops, my running home—and when someone called me "Rambo" after Sylvester Stallone, I embellished with a foolhardy recount. But all anyone had to do was look at my tennis shoes, which had been brand new and bright white the previous week. Now they were scuffed, stained, and creased with dirt. Mom had spent good money, and I ruined them.

In *The Geography of Childhood*, Trimble talks of "middle childhood," between seven and twelve years old, when we learn in a "fresh, receptive, and playful way," our brains poised between "inner and outer worlds." He describes Paul Shepard's "ark of the mind," which kids load "with animals, with plants, with place." Those are the memories that will one day shape our adult lives, the stories we'll always tell, and likely romanticize. I don't doubt that such an ark exists, a youthful period when we take in our surroundings, when we're "a vessel for teachers, family, and peers to fill." After all, I discovered rivers and road trips. But I also think there's another ark, one of the heart that overflows when we're teenagers, less carefree than our predecessors in childhood. More self-conscious. Burdened. And I put that November night in there, my family's struggles alongside the zigzagging, because I can't separate the sound of my mother's voice from the silence of that long, long walk. I remember, too, how slowly I drank that beer, pining for a cheerleader who'd never leave her boyfriend. I longed, yearned, for another kind of landscape, not only a girl, but also less worry.

Two autumns later, I'd fill the ark with similar emotions during fraternity lineups at DePauw. As a first-semester freshman clad only in boxers, I often stood along a wall with my sixteen pledge brothers. Hazing was common at SAE, from getting pranked to slaving for upperclassmen, but what we hated most was being dragged out of bed at 2:00 a.m., when we were told to strip down, pale and freezing. Then we'd file downstairs into the dining hall, a dim chamber of cigar smoke and noiseless men. We'd stand along that wall for an hour or two, each of us, one by one, enduring ridicule.

As rites of passage go, lineups didn't hurt that much: "Your grades suck! You don't drink! Why are you here?" My lungs burned yet somehow I welcomed it. Perhaps the smoky room reminded me of my father's house—a haze of self-harm and not giving a shit. Still, one lineup did sting deeply, or rather the uncertain minutes after it had ended, when we were asked to share memories from a pledge-class road trip to the universities of Illinois and Miami of Ohio. As before, each pledge took a turn in the spotlight, though this time there were cheers, even clapping. There were stories about smoking joints with other SAE chapters, stories about puking and passing out. "Dude, you smell like ass" was high praise back then.

I stood uneasily near the end of the row, laughing, sure, but also tormented. What should I say? I thought as my turn approached. I hadn't drunk or smoked, let alone passed out.

"Your turn, Muse," a senior said. "What's your favorite memory from the road trip?" Putting it like that, the question seems healthy, men bonding over stories told time and again.

Maybe I felt like that in the seconds before I spoke, recalling our caravan across three states. My hatchback had raced in a furious line, down interstates, down backroads. Or maybe the room's lightheartedness had given me some kind of reassurance, some comfort they'd like my story too. No matter what, I may have thought, they'll clap.

"I like that we drove five hundred miles," I said. "My odometer ... I kept track. We crossed rivers, creeks, and cornfields. We stopped at a Waffle House. I had pancakes."

The room fell quiet, agonizingly quiet. My tale was out of step. My whole life was. No one shifted in his chair, and no one said a word, until a sophomore spoke up, slowly.

"Crazy Muse," he said from the shadows, and I recognized his voice without seeing his face. A shy, brawny, good-looking fellow. A star teammate I admired on the football field. I realize Scott Stone didn't mean to hurt me. He'd added levity to an uncomfortable moment. But that nickname, that identity, would stick. They all started calling me Crazy, even my pledge brothers.

By the time I met Mia in the months ahead, I was resigned to my image, if not proud of it. At some point I grew up, I guess, if only by thickening my skin. And later, on our trip down the West Coast, another gear shifted in my character. Even though our romance didn't last, Mia introduced me to the man I would become. Or maybe she reintroduced the child I'd been, wide-eyed and seemingly carefree, full of questions while crossing a big river, my finger tracing a line to the unknown. So after graduating from DePauw in 1991, I moved to Washington with Toni, another girlfriend, with Kerouac's books and others in my rucksack, including *The Practice of the Wild* by Gary Snyder. "The wild requires that we learn the terrain," Snyder explained, "nod to all the plants and animals and birds, ford the streams and cross the ridges, and tell a good story when we get back home."

Picture what those words meant to a twenty-two-year-old: validation, permission, escape. I could leave my clumsy college days in Indiana behind. I had a new journey, a new companion. But sure enough, Toni dumped me in Washington, beneath the rain, the nonstop rain, and I'd like to blame the guy who came between us, a mutual friend who'd been a cop in LA. Yet even then I knew I had a hand in our breakup. My nagging restlessness. My angst. I'd struggled to find a job that wasn't a dead end. I'd complained too much. I'd lost confidence.

Again, it was late March on the West Coast, and the highway lay ahead for the taking. I may have been rootless, even depressed, but I loaded my pack and headed south. I wore a flannel shirt and cranked up Pearl Jam—"All the love gone bad / Turned my world to black"—and in Oregon veered off I-5 to meander along the California coastline. At night I slept in my car, and each morning explored trails and tide pools. Then, brooding, I came up with a plan, a purpose that meant *keep driving*.

Gary Snyder, I thought, what if I visit him? What if I drive to UC Davis? A book jacket had said, "He teaches literature and wilderness thought." That's all I knew, and went for it.

The next morning I walked into admissions, asking for a catalog of faculty offices, and as my fingers skimmed through the English department, nausea nearly buckled my legs. "Gary Snyder, BA." Gulp.

Until that moment, it hadn't occurred to me that you don't need a PhD to be exceptional. Snyder had published a dozen books, one winning a Pulitzer Prize for poetry. What I admired most about him, though, wasn't his accomplishments but his path. He'd grown up on a Puget Sound farm and climbed "great snowpeaks," inspiring his first attempts to write poems. Later, he'd been a fire lookout, a trail crew worker, even a logger. He'd labored on a seagoing tanker, eventually studying Buddhism in Japan. And in the late 1960s, he'd returned to the United States, settling in the Sierra Nevada foothills. He'd built a house off the grid, naming it Kitkitdizze. He'd built a family, planted roots, dug in.

Unlike Kerouac, who'd succumbed to alcoholism decades earlier, Snyder was alive and well, still growing. He was my literary and environmental hero. Could I simply walk up and chat?

You bet I could—in the cramped annex that held his office. But outside his door was a line of students, books in hand, a bit pushy. Unsure of what to do, I got in line too but waved more walk-ups ahead of me, hoping to talk to Snyder in private, though I had no idea of what to say. A half hour passed, and I stood alone, the last figure in a narrow hallway. I could hear Snyder's voice, intellectual yet folksy, as my palms grew sweaty and pits leaked.

When I entered his office, he barely looked up, enough to peer above his bifocals. His beard was pointy like a leprechaun's, mischievous looking but stern. "Wilderness lit or poetry?" he asked. I said nothing, sensing impatience. "Which class next quarter? Why are you here?" He motioned toward a stack of papers.

Oh, shit, what terrible timing! I've interrupted, I realized, a busy professor. It got even worse as I stuttered, stammered, and fumbled my words. "Neither, sir, neither. Just drove a thousand miles to meet you." I shut my mouth, horrified. I was on the verge of throwing up. Who says drivel like that? Crazy.

Snyder removed his glasses and said, "Please have a seat." He leaned back in his chair. "That's quite a journey." Then he asked which plants were blooming in western Washington. Trillium, I may have answered. Red-flowering currant.

His office was exactly what I'd hoped for. A time capsule, really. Books, artifacts, photographs, including his arm around Allen Ginsberg, the Beat poet who'd introduced him to Kerouac in 1955, before the Six Gallery reading in San Francisco. But what I didn't expect to see was Snyder's weathered, thick-fingered hand, passing me a dog-eared draft of "Coming into the Watershed," an essay he'd soon publish in the *Examiner*. It explained bioregionalism, the notion of defining our lives by ecological zones—"porous, permeable, arguable," he wrote, "boundaries of climates, plant communities, soil types." And as we talked about river basins—the Ohio, the Columbia, his own South Yuba—we shared our love of diversity, how the character and culture of each landscape shift subtly from mile to mile. "A sense of place," Snyder called it, a concept I've studied ever since.

We talked for twenty minutes or so, until more students filled the hallway. When I stood up to thank him, he asked, "How did you know I'd be here? This is my first day back on campus after a year." The spring quarter would begin in two weeks. His students were lining the hallway to pick up readings.

"I didn't. I didn't know your schedule." I told him about the book jacket, about thumbing through the catalog. "It was a coincidence, I guess. Dumb luck."

Snyder laughed, I beamed, and we shook hands goodbye. Wandering had never felt so good. Life itself hadn't.

My wife will read this tale and say I'm unhappy, that I toil in rehashing the past. She won't be wrong. She deserves better, as did my girlfriends, most of them anyway. Truth is, throughout my life, I've wrestled with worry and regret, with disquiet, with discontent. A sense of failure creeps in whenever depression swells from seasonal changes or career woes or, more recently, the physical effects of aging. My fraying spine makes it difficult to sit for long, to travel, to endure office jobs. I'm writing this tale as I have to—standing.

Terry Tempest Williams wrote, "It has been said there are two stories in the world: an individual goes on a journey or a stranger comes to town." What if you are both of these characters, your life both stories? Maybe that's what I mean by an ark, not only of the mind, as Paul Shepard theorized, but also of the heart. The heart holds more than the mind. It yearns, craves, races with joy. And sometimes it breaks. In that ark are all of my coming and going, my breaking and remaking. My fraying. I understand the journeyer, but the stranger still eludes me. Perhaps the stranger is unhappiness itself, coming to town, digging in.

But this is where my wife is wrong: I am more than my discontent. Just look inside this ark! I see trails and tide pools, cornfields and pitch-black county roads. I see my mother's love. I see the loss of my father, the paper bag in his hand, my search for other men. I see Bruce Springsteen and Eddie Vedder. I see the Indigo Girls when they sing about "the upper echelons of mediocrity." I see my first Patagonia fleece, my first Nalgene bottle, my first hiking boots. I see Ed Abbey's *The Monkey Wrench Gang* and Aldo Leopold's *A Sand County Almanac*. And I see the television show *Northern Exposure*, which as much as anything sent me packing, sent me west. I see Chris Stevens, Cicely's DJ, building a massive catapult to fling a piano skyward as the whole town watches, wonders, and helps me pursue the possibility—the very idea—that such passionate, convivial people might actually exist. As my wife did. A park ranger. I married her beneath a canopy of cedar trees.

Look at this ark, I want to tell her. Look closer.

Or look at the salmon on our wall. Maybe it's not a gift from an old girlfriend, but the ark itself. It's more than scrap metal and recycled wood, old nails and speckles of gray and gold paint. It's more than a reminder of what first led me west, girl after girl, all the fraying. Maybe she knows I need it on the wall, ever present, ever near. Maybe she knows that worry and regret, joy and hope, burst my heart every day. Every damn day. Now that's a woman to run to, to hang on to, to call home. She welcomes me again and again and again.

Hours after meeting Gary Snyder, I was back on I-5, rounding Mount Shasta from the south. Beneath alpenglow on the volcano's glaciers, I drove in silence, veering northeast on Highway 97 toward the high desert of Oregon, toward pines and sagebrush, jackrabbits and coyotes. My destination was the small town of Bend, where Tom, my best friend from college, lived with Jessie, a California girl who'd been in the same sorority as Mia and whom we had visited three years earlier on our way to Los Angeles. A New Yorker, muscular from his wrestling days, with a gnarly scar on his left cheekbone, Tom had moved west about the same time I did, leaving behind his own sour memories of our fraternity. We hadn't seen each other in ten months, since graduation, but I knew he was scraping by—the educated poor, like me.

Around midnight, I arrived on the porch of their second-floor apartment, where Tom bear-hugged me and our laughter misted like pale white fireworks in the frigid air. He told me that Jessie was already in bed for the night and had to get up early for a marketing job. Tom needed to rise even earlier. He ran a chairlift at the Mount Bachelor ski area, had become a talented snowboarder, and rode his bike each morning, no matter the weather, to catch a shuttle bus up the mountain. It was a far cry from our final semesters on the dean's list back at DePauw, when we'd partnered to win the senior research award in psychology. Still, he looked happy, as I was that night. I had a new story.

As we pulled out the futon in their tiny living room, where I'd sleep for a few hours until they departed, I told Tom about my visit with Snyder, how lucky I'd been to catch him in his office. Tom knew enough about the poet and essayist to understand his importance to me, and as much as anyone, he'd watched me grow in recent years—through girls, poor grades, and awkward parties. His journey to manhood had mirrored my own. That's why his question surprised me.

"Remember that lineup our freshman year," he asked, "when everybody laughed about your odometer?"

Inside I sank, recalling the scene. Why bring it up? He'd stood there too, agonizing.

"Crazy Muse," I said, slipping a sheet over the cushion, trying to act nonchalant, as if our past had long faded.

"I know," Tom said, grinning. "Look at what you did this time. Amazing."

Tom nudged my shoulder with brotherly pride, then headed back to bed, back to Jessie. I savored his words while reading a map, checking my route before turning off the light. I was so young then, lost perhaps, but resilient. Did I realize what lay ahead? Does anyone? Only now, three decades later, do I understand there is no separation between the journey and the hoped-for destination, between feeling at home and feeling like a stranger in my own skin. There is no separation between who we are and who we will become from one season to the next. We have no choice but to go.

TRAILBLAZERS

"Use this," the apprentice said.

The young Navajo man had a long ponytail, black as coal, and wore plastic eyeglasses, also black. He handed me a white cloth that felt like a threadbare T-shirt, instructing me to rip a strip from it and pass it on to the next guy.

"Now what?" I asked, imagining some sort of bracelet.

"Tie that around your foreskin to seal your penis," he replied. "You can't drip any semen in the sweat lodge. It's a sacred place."

I hesitated, stunned.

Don't *drip?* I thought. Are we about to masturbate? I don't even have foreskin . . . wait, does everybody else?

I could've vomited, nearing panic.

"You heard him," Kurt said. "Come on, give me that thing."

Staring at the string I'd torn, I tossed the remaining cloth to my fellow graduate student. No turning back now. I shivered in the falling snow.

Reluctantly, I unzipped my Carhartt pants and fleece jacket, then turned my back toward the others, each of them undressing. The group included a medicine man and his student—friends of the Yazzie family, our hosts—and my four male classmates in the Audubon Expedition Institute, plus a new professor, also male. The air in early April was crisp—the sweet fragrance of juniper and piñon pine. At 6,300 feet in elevation, the trees huddled as snow-dusted clumps. I wanted to sneak through their branches to hide, to disappear. The Navajo Nation in northeastern Arizona looked surreal, like another planet.

"What if you don't have foreskin?" I whispered, leaning toward Kurt. He seemed eager to get naked, his pants below his knees. "I mean, how do you *seal* it?"

Kurt laughed and said, "Relax. We won't be graded on this." He pulled off his shoes and piled his clothes on a remnant of orange shag carpet. Several rugs lay near a water-filled trash can steaming in a crackling fire. The sweat lodge itself was little more than a hut, low slung, covered in clay. It looked woefully small for eight men, especially long-legged Kurt.

Six foot five with sun-bleached hair, he was at least a decade older than me, and I considered him to be a mentor, though we were drastically unalike. Kurt was a free-spirited Floridian who loved the Grateful Dead. I, on the other hand, was twenty-four years old, a Midwesterner who didn't party. And I'd never gotten naked with men, except in the shower after football games. Circumstances then had been cut and dried. You did your business, and moved on. Yet if anyone could get me through this, my new hippie friend could. Kurt chuckled, watching me fondle a pecker that may have been Earth's tiniest. I was frightened. I was freezing. My fingers felt like ice.

"Just wrap it like a present," Kurt said, revealing the progress he'd made. The fabric dangled against his pubic hair and the pale skin of his gangly legs.

I stared for a moment, dumbstruck, uncertain of what to say. He didn't have foreskin either but had managed to complete the task. His penis indeed looked like a gift, topped off with a bright white bow. "My wife would love this," he said. "I wish I'd brought my camera."

I looked around at the others in the group, each navel-gazing and shivering, until the medicine man walked toward the lodge, his butt dark and wrinkled like leather. Before lifting the blanket on the doorway, he shouted some kind of announcement. "Ya'at'eeh!" is what I remember, his hands rising with his voice. His apprentice told us to yell the same thing, to say "hello to the talking gods." The sweat, he said, was a religious ceremony—instructions, songs, prayers.

Despondent, I finished tying my bow, stripped off my clothes, and folded them beneath an outcrop. Yes, I folded them, I remember that: what little I could control. I may have been freezing, or merely embarrassed, or teetering on the edge of panic, but I knew I'd eventually step out of that lodge and want my underwear to be dry. A man's got his limits, I guess.

I walked to the entrance and yelled hello, my first words in the Navajo language. "Ya'at'eeh!" I said, greeting the talking gods.

Twenty-seven years ago, in the spring of 1994, I hopped "on the bus" for my second semester in graduate school. The country's young president, Bill Clinton, had given his first State of the Union address after signing NAFTA, the North American Free Trade Agreement. Economic boom times lay ahead, the rise of dot-coms and the stock market, but behind it all lay another kind of world defying the politics of optimism. In the days before I entered that sweat lodge, Nirvana's Kurt Cobain committed suicide. He put a shotgun to his chin in his Seattle home, and depression and heroin pulled the trigger. Far worse would be the headlines to come, announcing genocide in Rwanda, when the Hutus murdered eight hundred thousand Tutsis in the span of one hundred days. Sitting on the curb of an Albuquerque food co-op, I read about the massacre in a newspaper. What's real, I wondered, which world, mine in safety or theirs in terror?

Still, my own life wasn't so blissful that spring, but rather a trial in discomfort. Most mornings I'd rise in the gray dawn light from a sleeping bag covered with frost. For my MS degree, I lived out of a customized school bus carrying fifteen students and three professors, with hundreds of books on bungee-corded shelves, loads of camping gear, and musical instruments. Each of us kept a "personal space" in a cardboard box under a seat, and stored our clothes in a wooden loft suspended from the metal ceiling. That is, we could stand upright in one of three spots along the aisle—the front, where the faculty kept their belongings, or openings in the middle and rear. Suffice to say, we leaned over a lot, maneuvering from one seat to another, the tambourine sound of ten thousand objects jangling as the bus bounced along.

Given that memory, I realize we all were hippies, not only Kurt. He just happened to look the part with his scraggly beard and Birkenstock sandals. As for me, I had discovered Patagonia clothing—recycled oil products turned into fleece—and on most days I lived in three or four layers, brightly colored and color-coordinated. And if lucky, we showered twice a week, though I made sure to shave every day, twirling a brush in a coffee cup to lather my beard with soap.

Get this: I still use that brush more than two decades later. Call me a tree hugger, an environmentalist. Why waste aluminum cans? And like most tree huggers I wanted camaraderie, which led me to get on the bus. The Audubon Expedition Institute, or AEI, spent semesters exploring North America. AEI's buses roamed from coast to coast, exactly what I wanted in my twenties, from the humid hollows of the Great Smoky Mountains to California's fog-shrouded headlands. The previous autumn we'd traveled from British Columbia to San Francisco, studying a curriculum in environmental education. Ecology, geology, teaching methods. History, politics, food. Food especially, always food—what we'd purchase for group meals on Coleman stoves. Imagine spending hours debating what to eat, whether to buy organic, unprocessed, or locally grown.

Truth be told, as much as I'm conscientious today, back then all I craved was calories, anything to keep on bodyweight, anything to keep me warm. I didn't want hummus, couldn't stand tofu, and sure as hell hated tabouli. But since keeping fresh meat was impractical, the best I could do was beef jerky. Vegetarianism became a forced march. I submitted in the end, starving.

I know you're saying, "Big deal, Jeff! You applied for the program, took out loans." The thing is, you don't realize how we made our decisions: meeting after meeting to reach a consensus. Everyone had to agree, and not simply agree but talk. Actually, we had to listen, and by listening to each other, grow. "To live in community," the faculty said.

Note the lack of the article *a* or *the*, as in driving truck or building trail. A stickler for grammar, I couldn't stand the phrase, though the practice itself wore on me: to live in community was an ethic. So we'd sit in a circle for however long it took, each saying what she wanted or needed. I say *she* because most of our group was composed of women, women unlike any I'd ever known. Hairy-legged women who didn't care about makeup. Earthy, tough, passionate. Women tired of men always setting the agenda, eager for a new culture, new rules.

Feminism guided the program, which didn't occur to me until I stepped on the bus. I'd seen a two-year road trip in the school's brochure and had imagined lighting out for the backcountry. But I'd grown up with a single mother, so perhaps I was primed for the cause, though I have to admit that on the day of that sweat, I was glad the apprentice said, "No women." I'd felt like I deserved a break—a chance to pal around with guys—but I had no idea that palling around meant playing with my peter, naked. Ironically, I'd gotten used to bus life, to the manners and customs of womanhood, to slowing down when I wanted to hurry, to collaborating instead of dominating. Yet swiftly discomfort reappeared as I undressed and stood near the sweat lodge, my anxiety rising in mountain-sized goosebumps, stretching and stretching my skin.

Somehow Kurt made it look easy, both the penis string and life on the bus. He was funny, laid back, empathetic, and liked to knit wool hats and gloves. Knitting on the bus wasn't unusual, at least not among the women, as I recall, and it occurs to me now that that might have been my problem: I didn't know how to endure long meetings. Kurt, though, had a way of enjoying them, as if saying, "What's the rush? I can knit." He'd needle away on a sweater or a scarf, chiming in whenever it pleased him. Looking back, I suppose he was teaching me something, modeling a skill I'd yet to acquire. Some call it patience to tolerate delay. To Kurt, it meant finishing a hem.

One thing I remember about the hours before that sweat was feeling cranky and lethargic from being sedentary. We'd been camping in a hogan in Mr. Yazzie's backyard between short trips to learn from tribal members. We'd eaten fry bread with his wife and children, driven to Window Rock to meet local politicians, and spent a day with the Navajo Nation Environmental Protection Agency, discussing coal mining and overgrazing. Sitting around had made me stiff. Who wouldn't want to hike, to *move*? So when that young apprentice walked up after breakfast, his request immediately piqued my interest.

"I have a work project," he said. "I need male volunteers with strong backs." I stood up, grabbed my jacket, and didn't worry about the details. I jostled out the door, all smiles.

The deal, he explained, was that the guys on the bus could experience a sweat with a traditional medicine man, but to earn that opportunity we'd have to perform manual labor—"manly labor," I bantered goofily. The apprentice led us down a short trail to the lodge, instructing us to deepen the lodge's floor. He said the only way to get a bigger group inside was to remove stone and dirt using hand tools. One of my bus mates,

Jim, grabbed the pickaxe. He was wound up even more than I was. An athlete from sports-crazed Philadelphia, Jim grunted wildly, swinging it from his knees. Meanwhile, the rest of us worked outside, hauling limbs and chopping wood, and the apprentice put rocks in the swelling campfire, soon carrying them to the lodge on a pitchfork. Soon, too, the metal trash can was positioned, filled with water, and left to warm in the flames. We admired our handiwork as snowflakes began to fall, until the medicine man appeared without a word.

Sure enough, within minutes I was holding that string, the joke of manly labor turned on its head, and after wrapping my present as Kurt had suggested, I followed the apprentice to the lodge. I remember now the others let me go first— the first of the White men to step inside. I saw the rocks redden as I lifted the blanket. The Navajo elder huddled in the back. Then the heat hit me like a shock wave—heavy, clammy, disorienting. My forehead bumped a timber, shaggy and rough, as the ceiling sloped rapidly downward.

"Sit side by side," the apprentice said. I knelt down and scooted into place. My testicles sagged atop nylon fibers as my left thigh pressed against the apprentice's. Yet my discomfort with nudity was gone, and in its place rose fear. The heat seared, stifled, invaded my orifices, and I questioned whether I could last five minutes. I'd heard this experience could take hours; a sweat was sacred, after all—a ceremony. Suddenly, all I felt was suffocation. In desperation I leaned toward the door. But the others had begun lifting the blanket, yelling "Ya'at'eeh!" before entering. I cherished each pulse of clean, cool air as it slipped in, warmed, and disappeared.

Finally, the eight of us were pressed into formation, a semicircle facing glowing rocks. Kurt, coincidentally, had climbed in next to me, though he couldn't cross his legs or lay them flat. Instead, his left thigh sprawled over my right—gargantuan, wriggling, wet. The best I could do was mumble at him, pushing and punching his kneecap. Everyone else's words also vanished, overcome by throat clearing. The stink and sweat gushed from our bodies, soaking the carpet, soaking the air. I know now that's the point—draining the flesh helps purify the mind—but all I could think about was trying to survive. Terrified, I began to pray.

How long can this go on? I thought. How long, in this heat? I leaned forward, legs pretzeling, hips pulling from their sockets, and craved the cooler air at ground level. Then the medicine man started singing his songs. Navajo songs. Incomprehensible. He chanted, chanted, on and on. I kept stretching, pretzeling, praying.

Good God! I thought, like a naïve bigot. Shut this guy up! Get me out of here! But no one spoke a word as the elder raised his voice, his song another body crowding the lodge.

Seconds became minutes, then a blur. Red rocks danced. Walls shook. I'm passing out, I thought. I can't take this. God help me! Stretch! Stretch!

Kurt, of course, kept wriggling all the while, his slimy leg now bashing my head. Half delirious, I pointed my bare ass skyward, having shifted to all fours like a wild animal. Still, I was surviving—that's all that mattered. Panic was behind me, as was dignity. My nose was on the ground, on the bottom of the sweat lodge. I had crawled to new territory. I could breathe.

The next spring, while interning with an environmental nonprofit, I was living in downtown Portland, Oregon, with my artsy girlfriend, Sophie, a Dutch-Indonesian Californian who fancied a Hoosier. We'd met on the bus, the same time as Kurt, and had bonded during a third-semester backpacking trip on which we both wore the same clothes for a week. One sunny noon, during my lunch break, we walked through Portland's Pioneer Courthouse Square as a boisterous, flag-waving parade happened by, dancing, hollering, rocking out. And it made me smile so effortlessly that my shoulders swayed with the music, my head bobbed, and I giggled. How happy I was, how grateful, grateful not only for my winsome girlfriend but for marching men, for flag wavers—tall, short, skinny, fat. They wore officer hats and nipple rings, spiked collars and leather pants. Butt-less black leather pants.

"Chaps," Sophie said. "What cowboys wear." She mentioned her uncle in Seattle.

Ah, I thought, new rules. Pioneers. Trailblazers.

And I understood in that moment that I was breaking trail myself, through an inner landscape, my own limits, as well as a new career. Two years later, after Sophie and I split up, I took my master's degree up I-5 to help create an environmental learning center. One of the project's leaders was the superintendent of North Cascades National Park, a towering man who commanded much respect. Once, he asked about my long-term goals, if I planned to teach, manage, or do something else. I'm unsure how I answered him, but I recall his advice on personal growth. He said to picture myself inside a circle, its boundary representing my comfort level. "Everything inside is what you're good at. Everything outside is your potential." He explained that the key is to keep expanding, to stretch my circle beyond discomfort. "Little by little, you can master new territory. Enjoy it for a while, then stretch again."

As I listened to the superintendent's earnest counsel, I couldn't help but think of Kurt inside that sweat lodge, how we'd shrunk and slithered and wrestled in the heat, our bodies banging together, gushing. And I remembered how everyone in the lodge that day had been surprised when the medicine man stopped singing, when he spoke in perfect English, the first we'd heard: "It's hot in here! I need a break!" Who knew the old man had been overheating, let alone the bigotry of our assumption. He told us to climb out, one by one, our bodies glistening, steaming, unfolding. The snow was falling thicker and faster now, so we shook off the carpet squares and stood upright. We cracked jokes about our smell and fussing with our penis strings as the elder and his apprentice poked fun at us.

That's when, I'd wager, my circle expanded, when my comfort or potential or the old rules stretched. I'm not saying it felt erotic, but rather primal, or elemental. I watched two guys take a leak without turning around. Others stretched their hamstrings, touching their toes. And the apprentice grabbed a milk jug with its top cut off, scooping water from the trash can to pour over himself. The rest of us followed suit atop a flat boulder, the liquid streaming down our taut bodies. I'm still amazed we all stood there, chatting in the snowfall—Indigenous men, White men, buck naked.

Our sweat would continue for another hour or two, though we could pass through the entrance as we pleased. I chose to linger outdoors, lying by the fire, pouring water on my skin to stay warm. Kurt, too, sprawled on the orange carpet, and we talked and laughed and retied our strings. At that moment, I'm sure, we thought little of the outside world, nothing of terror or depression or boom times. If anything, we talked about bus life, what the women were up to that day. Living in community was rarely comfortable or easy, but as Sophie would later say, I was growing. Who knows, maybe we made tofu that night. Maybe it was tabouli, and I starved. Looking back at those meals, I see the coward I once was. A real man, I know now, stretches.

DEER'S EARS

How do we become who we are in the world? We ask the world to teach us. But we ask with an open heart, with no idea what the answer will be.

— PAM HOUSTON, *Deep Creek*

Reba McEntire had spotted a woodcock. Named after the famous country singer with curly red hair, the hunting dog pointed her snout, trembling, and inched silently toward her prey. Her owner, George Darey, stopped walking and aimed his twelve gauge toward the treetops. "Good girl," he whispered, unlocking his safety. I waited for the blast, the blood.

A woodcock is also a timberdoodle, a bogsucker, or a brush snipe. Cute names, I thought at the time. My field guide had described a long-billed bird with a short neck and squatty legs—the inland cousin of the coastal sandpiper. Its plumage would match the drab pattern on the ground surrounding our dew-soaked boots. I scanned the terrain ahead of Reba and saw nothing but fallen leaves, the hues of brown, pale gray, and rust the perfect camouflage for mid-autumn.

Darey gave his Brittany spaniel time to do her job; he wouldn't fire at a bird he flushed himself. A fellow hunter coiled several yards away, and I stood back, covering my ears. "Good girl," Darey said again. I cringed, staring at his trigger. And I thought about another man, the Alaskan anthropologist Richard Nelson, who'd studied the Koyukon people for years, pursuing deer and other game alongside them. The Koyukon believe an animal will give itself, Nelson wrote, once a hunter has a history of respecting it. It's called luck, not skill, when the hunt is successful, which made me wonder, whose luck are we talking about?

The leaves rattled and stirred right in front of us, and then . . . whoosh! A tiny dark body exploded toward the sun in a blur of wing beats and shrill chatter. But neither hunter took aim, let alone fired, through the dense tangle of wiry limbs. It all happened so fast they couldn't position themselves to ensure each other's safety, and mine. Crouching, I had the perfect angle for a photo, though my fingers plugged my eardrums instead. Darey shook his head when he saw me wincing there, the reporter afraid of his own story.

"Sorry," I said. "Thought we had him." Lucky bird. Wimpy man.

That embarrassing hunting trip took place in October 1996, when I was twenty-seven years old, a year out of graduate school, studying environmental education and conservation. I was living with Sophie, my girlfriend at the time, in bucolic and scenic Great Barrington, a small, steeple-dotted town in the southwestern corner of Massachusetts. We'd settled there after working in New York on the nearby Hudson River, where we'd taught on a historic sailboat from Albany, West Point, and Yonkers to the Twin Towers on the tip of Manhattan. And while Sophie had found an administrative job at Jacob's Pillow, a dance festival and school, I took a stab at freelance journalism with a pocket notebook and point-and-shoot camera. Writing about hunting was one of my first assignments for the lifestyle section in the *Berkshire Eagle*, after the editor had handed me Darey's phone number, scribbled in red ink on a scrap of newspaper.

George "Gige" Darey was a lifelong resident of Berkshire County and the chair of the state's Fisheries and Wildlife Board. "But more importantly," the editor said, "he's one of the best sportsmen in Massachusetts." My job was to depict Darey positively in 1,200 words, to make hunters and hunting look good for the sake of local tourism. But even though I had acted professionally when accepting the assignment that afternoon, I walked away feeling conflicted because killing animals turned my stomach. As for hunting, I'd always feared it. Feared the guns. Feared the noise.

Indeed, as I crouched behind Darey, his shotgun poised skyward, a childhood memory emerged as I flinched, waiting for the blast. I hadn't shot at any animal myself for nearly twenty years, since I was a boy on my father's heels near his birthplace in southern Kentucky. In hardwoods much like the Berkshires, we pegged squirrels with a .22 rifle, each shot echoing like a firecracker as a fluffy tail fluttered to the ground. I remember picking up a squirrel I'd killed, its body limp yet warm and delicate, how blood smeared across my fingertips, how we would skin it from the bottom up. I cried about what I'd done, and couldn't stand the thought of eating it. As much as I would study nature one day, my heart was schooled right then.

"You don't have to become a hunter," Dad said, "but you need to see things like this." I looked closely as he instructed, but did we see the same thing?

I've always been emotional about animals, whether or not guns are involved. I feel regret for the things I've killed; at times I've had nightmares. All my life I've been drawn to creatures—pets, strays, wildlife—and even as a boy I knew that everything dies, often painfully, often tragically. I suppose that's what haunts me, the way animals look as they perish. I suppose there's a question we all need to ask: Do we die a little, too, when something passes?

Maybe it's due to my first memories of animals, though, really, they're family stories. It starts with a rooster my father killed, which I don't recall seeing happen. During one of my first visits to Kentucky, when my great-grandparents lived on a farm, I stepped from the car and ambled toward the chickens, saying, "Here, doggy, doggy. Here, doggy." One of the cocks reared up, squawking madly, thrashing its wings, and then I screamed bloody murder, running with my hands on my face. Decades later, I can point at my cheek where the rooster hacked with its spurs, and each morning as I shave I imagine the bird, kicked and kicked by my father. "Down a hill," Mom says, "feathers flying."

Next is our black poodle, Crybaby, whom we buried beneath a row of pine trees, though again it's just a family story, not something I remember firsthand. Still, Crybaby hangs over me, if not in memory, then as myth. Is that enough to shape a kid's heart, to make death as familiar as kin?

But there are others I do recall, including Ginger, our Irish setter. A deep-voiced man who lived two houses down shot her for crossing his lawn. I remember, too, our outdoor cats, most killed by passing cars. Toes, in particular, had oversized paws, like a catcher's mitt, wide and soft. One morning he followed me down the driveway as I walked out to catch the school bus, and then he darted headlong into the road, spooked by the screeching brakes. In tears I asked the driver to wait as I dragged Toes by his tail. He lay on the pavement with shiny eyes, mouth agape, tongue bleeding. I buried him when I got home from school, not far from Crybaby's gravesite.

Farther from our house in Indianapolis, numerous animals stand out, from a frog I crushed with a cinder block to a turtle that swallowed my fishing hook. And once, biking alongside a cornfield, I heard the gurgled cries of a hidden cat, and when I said, "Here, kitty, kitty," it appeared, missing half its neck. As I stared at the pus-filled cavity, the exposed muscles buzzing with gnats, the purring, orange, emaciated creature lovingly buttered my legs. I rode away, ashamed. The cat chased me, meowing.

Like much in my memory, though, our trips to Kentucky linger, as if the hot, humid, wilder South was a Noah's Ark for my imagination. Dad once took me to a pig slaughter, with its snorts and squeals and sausage grinders. Six or seven at the time, I peered up at flatbed trailers—hogs' heads on one, innards and hindquarters on others. I walked toward a wood-fired kettle, its contents simmering and pungent, and knelt down to pick up a strange object, the two-holed pad of a pig's nostrils. No blood, just squishy. Like Styrofoam or a piece of leather.

Yet one memory from Kentucky still haunts me, when my father ran over a dog near a cousin's house along Pitman Creek. It was a neighbor's elderly bloodhound. Calm, curious, sweet. Earlier that day I'd stroked its back as its tail thwapped rhythmically against my waist. I recall feeling a clunk on the floorboard, and a second clunk farther back—that moment when just-a-dog barking turns into squeals and yelps. Dad looked over his shoulder, swore, and shifted into park. Then he told me to stay put as he stepped out into the dust. I watched him through the rear window as an old man in coveralls approached, both of them lowering to comfort the animal, though appearing to say little to each other. Sullenly, the man walked back to his house, crossing a dilapidated footbridge, only to return with a silver pistol and still visibly upset. When he handed the gun to my father, I knew what to expect and dreaded it. The fiery blast made me jump with fright. The dog's body fell flat.

Back in the Berkshires, Darey loaded Reba into his pickup truck parked at roadside, the cab smelling of gun oil and a wet but much-loved spaniel. As I wrote in my notebook, he began telling stories about the uses for the animals he killed, pointing to a fly-fishing lure pinned to a cap on his newspaper-covered dash. The lure's deep-green feathers once colored a wood duck's head, but now, tied around a hook, they resembled the wings of a mayfly. "A trout's favorite meal," Darey said.

I realized then he was like my father, close to animals but killing them, and that he ate what he killed guilt-free as my fake meat traveled thousands of miles. Which is better, what kind of eating, local game or industrial veggie burgers? Whatever bias I had felt early on began to wane as we drove toward home. Darey had integrity and skills beyond my years, more than I could possibly write about. To help explain why hunters hunt and how a gun could offer more than death, I centered my article on self-sufficiency—putting food on the table for your family.

But reading it now, in my fifties, it's my article that seems fake. Back then I was trying to be a man, to fit in by embracing hunting. If I couldn't fire a gun, I figured, the least I could do was write about it. I could champion killing to put food on the table, though my own meals would pass through time zones. I don't so much feel like a hypocrite as I do a sentimental bleeding heart. If there's any reason I'm an environmentalist, it's due to my memories of animals—how they bent and broke and suffered, how they faded, how they perished. Darey and my father may have been right, but I grew up to be neither man.

Nonetheless, I'm still trying.

When I began crafting this essay—for a second graduate degree, in creative writing, I was living along the Upper Mississippi River, teaching environmental studies to college kids. My students came from small towns and paved-over suburbs and often spoke of their family cabins, some rustic spot beside a cerulean lake or deep in the woods among wildlife. And as with Darey and my father long ago, hunting came naturally for many of them. They talked of tree stands, bag limits, and the season's first kill as casually as sharing their social lives.

How do I know? They wrote about it, and did so with passion and purpose. Each week they turned in a short essay about a course topic or outdoor experience. Their pens often turned to hunting. But more than dwelling on death, they wrote about sitting in a forest, how it felt to slow down and pay attention to nature—deer, turkeys, a bobcat. I envied them, I knew even then, for what they already seemed to understand, that death is indeed like kin, intimate and unconditional. The blood didn't seem to scare them the way it does with me, and sometimes I think they saw me as Darey did: a tree hugger, wincing and soft. In the least, they knew I was hitched to one.

Two decades ago, I married Paula, and we lived out west for many years, until circumstances led us to La Crosse, Wisconsin, for her job along the Upper Mississippi. Come fall, one of her most difficult duties was conducting bag checks of waterfowl hunters, and among many of the migrating species, wood ducks were often shot—hundreds in a single day. Paula would come home exhausted from the counting, a dark humor keeping her afloat. "If it flies, it dies," she said, shaking her head, recalling piles of bodies. Every time she told such a story, I thought about holding that squirrel. I thought about my students and their hunting essays, how they felt close to animals, how they killed them.

My wife, predictably, is just like me—an environmentalist, an animal lover. She enjoys watching and studying birds, including woodcocks and wood ducks. E.O. Wilson calls it *biophilia*—an inborn affinity for other life forms—but he also believes people can cherish animals while hunting, killing, and eating them. One way or the other, he said, we all play a part in the killing, if not directly taking a creature's life, then destroying its habitat to build our homes. Our cities, our highways, our shopping malls. Everywhere. Every day.

Wilson's idea, however, doesn't explain how I feel. The way I love animals is akin to the Latin root *anima*—"breath, soul, life force." I witnessed exactly that when my father shot that old man's dog, how it gasped and writhed and fell in the dust, lifeless beneath a wisp of gun smoke. "A mercy killing," Dad called it, as he shut the car door and drove on. I don't doubt that he saw it that way, though all I felt was regret. For the gun, the car, the things of man. A regret I can't seem to shake.

Or maybe what I feel on most days is the Japanese *mono no aware*, "the pathos of things." It's the melancholic beauty we experience in life when observing the transience of existence. In Wisconsin, I would feel it beneath October's frail leaves, a sky laced with migrants headed south. Like Reba, I had my eye on something, something fleeting, something impermanent. Pets, wildlife, my elusive father, all of them are long gone.

One evening I took out my notebook as Paula and I drove westward from La Crosse. We traversed the Upper Mississippi on I-90 and headed south beneath Minnesota's bluffs. Near Iowa we walked along Lock and Dam 8, which creates a lush, miles-wide marsh. As sunset waned, the rice beds darkened, providing nighttime shelter for wood ducks.

Each fall day, the birds take cover in the woods downstream of the earthen dam. They gorge on the acorns of swamp white oaks, fueling up to continue migrating. With a sweeping, showy crest, the males have red eyes and an orange, black-tipped bill. Imagine dark green, its most lustrous hue, to visualize the animal's head. Though camouflaged in mostly brown and gray, the females are equally beautiful, their feathers like leaves layered beyond count on a forest floor at the end of autumn. Both the males and females are smaller than mallards, and instead of quacking, they seem to squeak, like an infant's toy, soft and plush, high-pitched, even adorable. Is it wimpy to say that? After all, I've only heard wood ducks scurrying for their lives in flight. That night atop the dam, Paula and I froze as thousands lifted from the trees to the marsh. The sky was full of song, but what kind of song? Do others hear it? Do you?

"Try this," Paula said, cupping her ears to amplify the sound. "Deer's ears," she grinned, both of us looking silly. I once did the same thing with children at a YMCA camp. An environmental educator two months out of college, I hadn't a clue about anything. Was that really three decades ago? Am I that old, this fast?

I think about what had transpired during that year in Wisconsin, our lives racing by like those birds. My grandmother in Indiana lay on a months-long precipice before succumbing to pneumonia that winter. And Paula's brother in Connecticut had recently lost his wife to a heart attack at forty-seven. Though surviving for two weeks, she had suffered brain damage, and soon her anima slipped away. We were struggling with heavy hearts. Wisconsin was not home.

But standing on the dam that night, Paula and I kept up our deer's ears. Come dawn, we knew, a dozen hunters would appear, their shotguns poised skyward. Countless creatures were bound to perish, though we didn't feel anxious or sad. We weren't overwhelmed by troubling questions. Wood ducks are stealthy. Most survive. Still, that notion seeped into my mind about what happens when blood is spilled. We talked about our family and the animals we love, our voices rising in the moonlit mist. In time I took out my notebook and wrote a line or two beneath my headlamp. I thought of little dogs trembling and birds taking flight. I felt lucky. I felt alive.

THE MOON, THE RIVER,
A BEST FRIEND

August 28, 2007
Skagit River, WA

Ned and I started paddling at four o'clock this afternoon. An upriver wind chafed our faces as the milky green melt of four hundred glaciers carried us downstream. We meandered twenty-five miles from Rockport, under Concrete's steel Tinkertoy, the Dalles Bridge, then beyond the bluffs of Cape Horn, where the Skagit doubles back for a horizon-wide view of craggy Sauk Mountain, named for the *Sah-ku-méhu* tribe. Late summer withers the peak's avalanche chutes—tawny meadows, a hint of gold. Several miles later, at the old ferry crossing in Birdsview, we pulled ashore on this gravel bar, its beach woven with polished rocks and piles of bark-stripped logs. We ate cold pizza and watched the sun set. No tent. No hassle.

The dew is falling thick and fast, smearing these few words. Rising through the cottonwoods, a full moon casts the sand and driftwood around this camp in a shadow-carving glow. We settle into our sleeping bags on plastic tarps, curling the edges to protect our gear. It's no use. We know we'll wake up soaked.

"It'll be sunny tomorrow," Ned says, his last words for the night. Then I zip my bag around my body, the scrape of nylon giving way to water sounds, to rolling waves and eddies curling against the shoreline.

The moon, the river, a best friend. What feels like a best friend. Within weeks, he'll be gone, back to Idaho, back to Driggs. "It actually snows there," he once told me. Here, on this valley bottom, it mostly rains. And Ned doesn't like rain.

We're on our way to Skagit Bay—or so we tell ourselves. Come morning, stocking caps on, we'll shake off the dawn-wet chill like French Canadian voyageurs, taking breakfast after an hour or two in the canoe. Ned's got the broad shoulders of an athlete, though not from gym weights or ball fields, but from mountaintops, sheer cliffs, places I don't go. He may not know it, but I'm giddy, thrilled that the paddle in his hands is adventure enough for his days off. I supervise him at work, but rarely does it feel like that. I hired him, I told my boss, "because this place needs a Ned." Our plan came together only last night as our schedules and aspirations aligned for the first time this summer. We're thriving on the spontaneity of the trip, the uncertainty around each bend. "A quick journey," I promised my wife. She shoved us off, waved.

All told, we'll cover some seventy miles from my house in Rockport to the Skagit Delta on Puget Sound. If the wind and tides will let us, if our backs hold out, we'll hit saltwater by early evening tomorrow. Thanks to her cell phone, a friend from headquarters will meet us wherever we end up—Mount Vernon, Fir Island, the Swinomish Channel in La Conner. "Just call me," she said. "I've got a truck, plenty of room."

But Ned and I agree—about paddling, about life—we want the sea. We want what glaciers want. We want as far as we can go.

FROM FIRE LOOKOUTS
TO SLAVE CABINS

The lightning stool sits by the counter, evidence that I
am not yet convinced that the storm is over. There are
little puddles outside where the hail was blown into piles
by the wind. She blows strongly still and the sky to the
north periodically flashes with light. So it has been and
continues to be a rather exciting morn'. I am grateful for
this tiny pagoda. Water's boiling. Time for tea.

—PAULA OGDEN-MUSE
Copper Ridge Lookout, August 6, 1991

A fit, gray-haired maintenance foreman for North
Cascades National Park, Ray was one of my favorite
neighbors in the densely forested Upper Skagit Valley,
where I managed adult field programs for North Cascades
Institute and later its campus in the park. A precarious
century had begun—the long years of Bush versus Gore, 9/11,
the wars in Afghanistan and Iraq, and a nationwide recession
that eventually hammered our own operation. Lost revenue.
Furloughs. But seeing Ray usually helped—his rural cool, his
ease, a disarming charm that relaxed anyone who spent time
with him, if only a moment's passing. Motioning toward me
to say hello, he'd clasp my hand with his elbow bent and

fingers curled, as if wanting to arm wrestle, and then lower his voice to a near growl. "How you doing, buddy?"

I'm sure he said those words to everybody, but in my early days of settling in Marblemount with Paula—"Ranger Paula," as many people called her because she wore a uniform on the job—I'd shake Ray's hand and feel the wiry hair on the back of his knuckles, and admire the cuff bracelet on his tanned wrist, a sturdy copper band with intricate markings. It reminded me that I could be both masculine and creative, hardscrabble and adorned. And I felt special, talking to Ray. I felt at home. I felt like, as he said, a buddy.

Before retiring in 2011, the year after Paula and I left the Upper Skagit due to a whole mess of bullshit that would lead to her suing the National Park Service for discrimination, Ray had been the most senior employee at North Cascades, having worked on Ross Lake since before the park's creation in 1968. I haven't seen Ray since we left, but it's safe to say he's still an artist and naturalist who loves good stories and wild places. And in the early 1970s, after graduating from college, he was a firewatcher in the fourteen-by-fourteen-foot lookout cabins on Desolation Peak, Copper Ridge, and Sourdough Mountain, all still maintained by the Park Service, all part of the country's wildland fire surveillance program before there were helicopter surveys and satellite imagery.

"Ray's the real deal," I used to say. When he described how on lookout, "every day, all the time, those mountains look different," I understood, if only by witnessing how the memory moved him. I laughed, too, whenever he talked about his first stint on Desolation—with little food, no entertainment, and a monk's idealism. Or later, on Sourdough, when he was looser and wiser, he counted on a Cessna pilot he knew only by radio to drop ice cream and beer on nearby snowfields. "When a can busted on impact," Ray would say, "you'd hustle to suck down the brew, on the clock or not."

I often reflected on his tales as I pulled into the environmental learning center's parking lot along the rocky shore of Diablo Lake. The fifteen-building campus sits at the southern foot of Sourdough Mountain, five thousand feet below the lookout and one reservoir downstream of Ross, and as I stepped into my office—the director's office, roughly the size of a firewatcher's cabin—I wondered what my life might have been like had I traded all my paperwork for a logbook, my computer for a walkie-talkie. What might it mean to be the real deal, I thought, an authentic North Cascades original? Ray, I suppose, was my muse.

For ten summers, in mid-August, Ray and I taught an Institute field seminar called Beats on the Peaks: Lookout Poets and Backcountry Tales. By boat, we'd traverse Ross Lake between Sourdough and Desolation, about fifteen miles apart. Gathering schoolteachers and history buffs, retirees and outdoorsy couples, we'd hike across Ross Dam to board a barge Ray had captained for decades—the *Mule*, its back saddled with a picnic table and a few folding chairs. "A floating classroom," he called it, when he wasn't hauling a load.

Camping three days at lakeside, we'd study fire scars, the ways of wildlife, how mountains and rivers form, and celebrate Gary Snyder, Jack Kerouac, and the long line of scribblers who'd spent time in the North Cascades for labor and adventure. We'd talk about wilderness rangers and trail crew, horse packers and dam builders. And firewatchers, naturally, including their Osborne firefinder, a compass-like turntable mounted in the center of a lookout. Joking about the weather, Ray would reminisce about hopping on the cabin's miniature stool, which was insulated with glass footings. "Every lightning storm," he'd say, "I was scared shitless. Every time."

Saturday mornings, we'd rise early for the hike up Desolation Peak, where Kerouac stood watch in 1956, a few months before publishing *On the Road*. "Expect a full day's journey," I'd tell our students. Twelve miles round trip, a thigh-burning climb up 4,500 feet. Then we'd race down dozens of switchbacks to skinny-dip in Ross Lake.

Later, after dinner, we'd huddle around the firepit to fill journals with snippets for next-day poems: off-color remarks, our raging blisters, the vanilla-scented ponderosa pines we'd pressed our noses into. Or how thrilling it had felt to visit the uniformed firewatcher on duty, seeing her tidy bedroll and an unassuming writing desk topped with paperbacks, including *The Dharma Bums*, which we'd passed around to read out loud, to relive it. And in those moments near dusk, the tree trunks in shadow, I'd point out Nohokomeen Glacier—pink, rock-rimmed, what Kerouac had called "a hundred football fields of snow."

I cherished each lingering, sap-crackling campfire, how Ray and I always stayed up late. Our students lay in their tents, exhausted, most fast asleep, one or two with headlamps still glowing. The fire's embers would fade, the smoke would shift, and we'd say little if anything at all. I loved how simple it was, waves lapping against the *Mule*'s metal hull. Quiet. Mountain-quiet. The stars oblivious to winter's rain. I felt like the most important person in the world—Ray's buddy. I felt rooted. I felt like a tale in the making in my own right.

In reality, I've written this tale several times, even published it. The original essay, a few paragraphs, won a *High Country News* contest called "Stories of the Working West." Readers liked the affectionate narrative, loved Ray and Snyder and Kerouac. "You created a literary landscape," someone on Facebook commented. But what I wrote ten years ago reveals the paean I was telling myself—a sugarcoated fond farewell. It expresses none of the turmoil that forced our departure, none of the anger, regret, or loss, and I can't pass it on unchanged. Because I've changed. The memories. The meanings. The way

I feel about the place and the people and that time—it's all changed. I was a boy then, and a boy idolizes, craving to fit in.

This largely has to do with how Paula was treated by her last set of supervisors at North Cascades National Park, and by some of my coworkers at North Cascades Institute. As the park's nonprofit partner, the Institute is responsible for operating the environmental learning center, which was designed and constructed with public funding. I'm thinking mostly of men who also called my wife "Ranger Paula," usually warmly, though at times mockingly, as when one of our male graduate students remarked about her "costume." Nonetheless, the Institute relied on her expertise as the only Park Service employee and emergency medical technician based on campus. We counted on her presence until, as one of my former friends and a manager from headquarters put it, "I hate your wife." He hated her because she had not forgiven him for a workplace disagreement on which legally I shouldn't elaborate, even though he'd also say "I hate Paula" to Ray, a nonvoting member of the Institute's board of directors. Ray, in the weeks ahead, told me about their conversation, but he never stepped in, even though Paula would later ask him for help.

As I said, this eventually led to a lawsuit, after Paula had been removed from the environmental learning center and I had resigned. Her supervisors had reassigned her to the park's nearby visitor center but ultimately denied her a promotion due to a trumped-up performance evaluation, the first and only one of her career. Her performance, as it were, was dependent on her relationship with the Institute, including the manager she had aggrieved. His badmouthing had persisted, which not only dashed her prospects but nearly ruined our marriage. And for that, the blame is mine.

What I mean is, I blame myself for working so much to launch that multimillion-dollar campus inside the park. I missed dinners at home, missed neighborhood walks, missed opportunities to hold hands, dig in the garden, and enjoy the house Paula and I had built in a five-acre patch of horse pasture, its tall grass undulating in an upriver breeze that was especially lovely come August. I blame myself for confiding in others, including my former friend who knew well the tension in our marriage, my second thoughts, my coming to terms with not having children, which, as I later discovered through counseling, I wanted no more than a purpose in life beyond my job. Hell, I blame myself for pursuing that position at the environmental learning center—the site director role, supervised from downvalley—when I knew the Park Service had long planned to station Paula in that location. That meant we would work together every day. That meant our marriage *was* our jobs. That meant my midlife doubts would not only fracture Paula, fracture her like ruthless ice, but do it in front of everyone. I realize now there is no place for a woman who doesn't smile. If she's not pleasing people, they ostracize her, as I shamefully tried to do. I bought into the bullshit that Paula had brought all these problems onto herself, that she was too rigid, too unforgiving, that her standards were too high both as a ranger and as a wife.

And so I blame myself for stories, for perpetuating and fueling them, which contributed to the misogyny Paula experienced. Stories have a power that only now, as a middle-aged man, I seem to comprehend. Stories often start before us, are bigger than us, and go on long after we're gone. And stories too often directed at women can be personal, hurtful, and sometimes you don't know the hurt until years later, when it all adds up—the characters, the plot, the climax. The loss of a house, a community, roots.

For instance, Ray shared a seemingly innocuous story at our wedding reception in September 2002, long before the opening of the environmental learning center. He stood before our family and friends and talked about knowing Paula since the eighties, watching her grow, watching her through several relationships with men he knew well. The Upper Skagit is a small community, after all, mostly parkies. I fathom now that as Ray talked he'd known Paula since her time as a backcountry ranger in the park's Wilderness District, before a climbing accident had shattered her ankles. The accident occurred during her graduate studies with Western Washington University and was caused by the negligence of a male professor who had helped found North Cascades Institute. He failed to secure the belay, which meant she tumbled to the ground when inevitably, as a beginner, she lost her footing. The professor hid behind lawyers, so Paula took the settlement and learned to walk again. That settlement money purchased the five-acre parcel on which our house was built years later.

As I stood next to Paula at our reception table, smiling at Ray, she wore slipper-like flats so as not to appear taller than me. The flats didn't provide ankle support in the way that her hiking boots did. Instead, they were feminine, sleek, pearly white, just like her dress, which had been embroidered with beads configured to look like dragonflies, one of her favorite creatures. I recognize now that she was in pain, standing there, as she had been while standing through our vows that afternoon. Those shoes have rarely left our closet since.

As for Ray's story, he told of Paula once being wooed by a man during a rafting trip down the Skagit River, a tale she'd shared with him years before, as a young woman. Along a leisurely stretch, Ray explained, the man began eating raspberries he'd purchased from Cascadian Farms, a local business. Paula watched as some of the berries went into his mouth and others, which he'd deemed undesirable, were tossed into the river. "He disrespected the Skagit," Ray said, "and that was that. Ranger Paula had seen enough."

"Well done, Jeff," Ray added, raising his glass for a toast. "You passed the raspberry test." The room erupted with laughter.

As luck would have it, a few weeks before our wedding and shortly before that season's Beats on the Peaks class, Paula and I spent a day on Ross Lake with Gary Snyder and a few friends, including Ray at the helm of the *Mule*. The previous afternoon, Snyder and Ray had spoken in a Park Service event called A Lookouts' Rendezvous, which honored John Suiter's photo-filled book, *Poets on the Peaks*, a first-rate history of Beat Generation writers in the North Cascades. It was the second time I had met Snyder but his first visit up the Skagit Valley in nearly half a century, and the first time he would travel north of Sourdough Mountain, seeing the lookout cabin from another angle, high atop a snowy ridge.

Aboard the *Mule*, as wind kicked spray across the bow, Snyder talked about the summers he'd spent firewatching in 1952 and '53, first on Crater Mountain, then across the lake on Sourdough. I told him how his poem "Mid-August at Sourdough Mountain Lookout" had inspired me to move west after growing up in Indiana, how I turned to it year after year, how Ray and I celebrated it with our students. He thanked me, smiling. We all smiled. It was a good day, one of our best.

"When you wrote those poems on Sourdough," I asked, "did you expect them to have such a lasting influence? Did you expect to impact all the people here?" I pointed around the boat and to the landscape beyond.

"No, I was just a kid," Snyder replied. At seventy-two, he gestured with wrinkled hands. They were tan, mole flecked, like his face, though his pointy beard made him look elf-like. "Those poems started out as journal sketching notes," he said, "with a little haiku mixed in." He'd developed the style from the Chinese poetry he was studying at the time. "Are you familiar with Han Shan?"

Snyder described the ninth-century Tang dynasty poet who lived in a place called Cold Mountain. I was familiar with the man from Snyder's early translations but had never really grasped the history. Han Shan was part of a long line of Chinese poets who wrote about the hermit's life. Their words trailed across centuries. Their words trailed through each other.

Finishing his explanation, Snyder looked at me as if waiting for a nod. But I needed to hear more.

"You see," he said, "ours is a baby culture." His thumb veered toward the lookout above us. "We'll need a hundred poets on Sourdough and a thousand other peaks to be rooted here, or anywhere. I was only one."

And I was another, I gathered. In my own way. In my own time.

Later that afternoon, Snyder relaxed alone, his elbows on the railing, and Ray stood at the helm as friends leaned in close to talk over the diesel engine. Maybe I knew then that this is how it works, rooting yourself in a place, in a community, slowly but surely, like the pace up Desolation or Sourdough, up switchbacks that never seem to end. It can take years to find a home, years to settle into a marriage. It can take years to figure out who you are, what matters to you, and why. What I couldn't have known then, and I'm still trying to figure out, is how I'd end up rewriting this essay in South Carolina, three thousand miles from Ross Lake.

Today, in Charleston, I often rise early to read a book or work on my own writing. Then I depart for my job as an interpretive guide at a former cotton plantation, focusing on African American history, racism, and the Black and White families who lived on the site for generations, until early 1990, my junior year in college. The stories climb through slavery, the Civil War, Reconstruction and Jim Crow, the civil rights movement and beyond, but seldom does a day go by, as I talk with throngs of tourists, as well as descendants, that I don't think of Beats on the Peaks. I think of Ray. I think of firewatchers and their tiny cabins.

The preserved wood-plank dwellings at McLeod Plantation Historic Site are approximately the size of the mountaintop pagodas I hiked to for years. Their histories are vastly different, of course, though I've come to know both intimately. My career has swung from fire lookouts to slave cabins, from celebrating isolation by choice to interpreting exile by force. The austere buildings were occupied not by solitary White men reading books and scribbling poems, but by eight, ten, a dozen or more people, Black families for whom reading and writing were outlawed during bondage. And during the violence and discrimination of the Jim Crow years, such as 1952 and '53, when Snyder was on lookout three thousand miles away, the cabins housed hardscrabble tenant farmers raising "truck crops" for distant markets, and raising children they'd send off to a segregated school, a three-mile walk from the plantation. Immense, moss-draped live oaks would haunt that walk, their stout limbs symbolic of a "hanging tree." "Whites Only" signs would haunt that walk, an ever-present reminder of who belongs in one place and not in another.

I never expected to learn about slave cabins and to draw inspiration from those who dwelled in them—a lesson in perseverance, or how to live through being severed from what you know and what you love, then thrust into exile, rootless. But as soon as I write that, I realize how naïve it sounds. I'm a White man, unbound. How can I possibly grasp what the people at McLeod Plantation went through? And yet I reach for it. I dig in. I lead hourlong tours through family stories.

Explaining how I ended up in South Carolina can be a straightforward answer, and usually it is when a visitor inquires after one of my tours, having heard my nonlocal accent or my references to other places. "My wife and I moved to Charleston for her job with the National Park Service," I say. "I started working here because I wanted to learn this history."

But that's a half-truth, really. A white lie. I never *wanted* this. It's not that this history didn't interest me, but rather slavery, the Old South, and the journey of African Americans through so much hardship—a journey of profound courage and strength—had seemed otherworldly, a part of the American story far removed from my interests among mountains and rivers and ponderosa pines. Yet my path has led here. And here my wife is, now a Park Service manager, a chief. Paula supervises all the interpretive rangers for Fort Sumter and Fort Moultrie National Historical Park and Charles Pinckney National Historic Site, a complex that receives nearly one million visitors each year, hundreds of thousands more than the North Cascades operation. Sure enough, she leads with a kind of "raspberry test"—high expectations and high accountability—while supporting her staff in ways she didn't experience during our final years in the Upper Skagit. And by support, I mean respect.

I see courage and strength in her as well. That is, when I see her depart for work each morning—uniform pressed, flat hat level, hiking boots on no matter the weather—I know she is stronger than any story used against her, any story about being too rigid, too cold, too unsmiling, a story too many women of any color have heard from far too many men, including their husbands. If there's a tale to celebrate here, it's one of resilience. My wife is tough, far tougher than I am.

"We can't look back," Paula tells me. "*I* can't." She doesn't even want to read this essay, proofing it, reliving it. But we are not at home in Charleston—few friends, no buddies, rarely an old-timer who greets us warmly. We are "from off," as lifelong residents say, at least some of the White ones I have met.

Although I'm proud of my wife's perseverance, and for that matter, my own, we toil beneath the weight of loss, even as we take inspiration from those who dwelled here before us, those who dwelled here against their will. And I've come to understand that what I do each morning, writing, parallels my work as a historical interpreter, always looking back, always interrogating. Memories. Meanings. America's narratives, her tales. Every day, it seems, when I help tourists break through the *Gone with the Wind* façade of what had actually been a slave labor camp, I feel myself doing the same, turning the lens on my own stories: boys' clubs in literary movements, national parks as idealized landscapes, even preserved wildlands, which often have not been preserved without removing those deemed undesirable, particularly Indigenous communities.

Even so, I catch myself romanticizing other places, or a place where I did feel at home once. I think of Bellingham, for example, a short drive from the Skagit Valley, where I chose to settle after college, before meeting Paula. I think of the sulfurous Georgia Pacific paper mill, of salmon flashing in midcity creeks. I think of the Bagelry's strawberry schmear and steam-soaked windows streaked with rain. I think of wet tires whirring, gulls calling, trains blaring along the waterfront, and a muddy bike trail beneath cedar boughs, my backside caked with splatters. And I think of a clear day when Mount Baker was out, or *Kollia-Kulshan* to the Nooksack tribe: "white, shining, steep mountain." I miss it. I miss all of it. The opposite edge of the continent. I first landed there in 1991, jobless and unbound.

Now, years and years later, I try to convince myself that I've changed, that counterculture writers and lookouts and an old Park Service barge don't matter anymore. But my bookshelves are lined with Beat Generation titles, and the images on our walls are entirely Cascadian. I see the rings on our fingers, each sterling silver, each etched with the view from Copper Ridge Lookout, where Paula summered as a backcountry ranger the same year I arrived in the lowlands. I also see the metal bracelet on my own wrist—sturdy, intricate, a man's thickness. I had stopped wearing it until recently. I had stored it away, with anger, regret, loss. With the betrayal of people who failed to stand up for Paula, including me, including Ray. How others embraced the young man who took her place, a man who soon left the park because he couldn't hack the remoteness, the isolation. He doesn't even wear the uniform anymore.

But today, as I rewrite this essay, wrestling with memories, with meanings, with passing a test or failing it, I slide the old bracelet back onto my wrist and it feels fine. It feels at home. It reminds me of what Snyder said on the *Mule*, that ours is a baby culture, that our lives are forever striving for sure footing, that our marriages are, and our friendships. I realize now this is a tale in the making, far from finished. It is not done, as I am not. As Paula and I are not done. Our roots grow and deepen and bind—in each other.

SAR TALK

August 28, 2008

Wilderness Office, Marblemount, WA

When I arrived for my shift this morning, a search and rescue operation, a "sar," was underway. Two climbers on Spire Point are stuck on an eighteen-inch ledge after losing most of their rope and camping gear—and now freezing. It's the remote tail of the Ptarmigan Traverse, a spot between Sentinel and Dome peaks most people reach only by mountaineering for several days. A fearsome crest. The *Pacific* Crest. Waters spill east toward the Columbia River or west to Puget Sound. Yet if you get high enough with a straight shot at a cell tower, your phone might work, as it did for those climbers this morning. They called 911, who in turn called us, the Park Service.

At least I gathered that, walking in. But what do I know? I can hardly handle my ice axe. It's my first season as a backcountry ranger, and probably my only one. I'm thirty-nine years old, too old to start this. Too slow. A plodder. I've got a decade or more on the other rookies, mostly college kids, a vet or two. They've come out west like I once did—poor, antsy, strong.

I hear chatter about the SAR in the backroom. "Cloud cover." "Window of opportunity." It's been raining for hours, and the snowline's dropping quickly. Those climbers might perish come nightfall unless we do something, unless someone with skills does something. Me, I'll be at this counter all day, saying, "Drive east on Highway 20. To the rainshadow. To dry trails."

The other rangers? Most are already in the backcountry. "On patrol," we say with self-importance. But a couple of the older, more experienced guys are stuffing overnight gear into their packs, prepping for a helicopter ride with Tony. I see their tan hands and best-job-ever grins, their colorful climbing boots, their colorful ropes. Soon they'll fly south to Darrington and up the Suiattle toward Bachelor Creek. From there it's a bushwhack beyond Itswoot Lake into cloud-shrouded terrain beneath Spire Point—a long slog over rocky ridges draped in slick heather and slush.

"Is it supposed to dump all weekend?" someone asks. A woman, two kids at her elbow. She's standing at the counter, annoyed.

"Yes, ma'am," I tell her, pointing to the forecast I put on the wall. She drags her kids over to read it, sighs, slumps her shoulders.

But the kids aren't annoyed, instead fixated—on our bear canisters, on our climber's log. One of them, a little boy, keeps watching me, his head owl-like over his shoulder. He makes me think of one of my nephews, the older one who's been out here. A bright blue shirt. A ball cap. His skin is bronze from a summer outdoors.

The counter is important, I try to tell myself. The lead ranger put me here because I'm good with people. I used to direct the environmental learning center but quit three months ago, tired of the long hours, tired of my boss, tired of how my wife got removed unfairly. I was caught in the middle, pissed. Now I'm just pissed at myself. Pissed at marriage. Pissed at failing. Pissed at no longer leading. I've got a shiny gold badge that looks like a toy. I've got a buzz cut, a thinning hairline. I'm in my own damn storm. On a ledge. Stuck.

The little boy steps toward me as his mother and sister talk with a man. Dad, I assume. His hair's dripping. The boy's head rises just above the counter, high enough to survey our topographic map. The map's pressed under glass, marked with symbols, and spreads farther than he can reach. He points and taps but doesn't speak as his fingers smudge the surface, perhaps as those climbers had done a few days ago, studying their route, imagining it.

The boy's movements keep my attention. His sleeveless arm. His probing hand. I lead him along the Ptarmigan Traverse to the edge of the counter near his nose. I read aloud the names of the peaks zigzagging along the Pacific Crest. "Mix-Up, Magic, Spider," I say, deepening my voice to sound tough. "Formidable, Old Guard, Spire Point." He looks up at me, wanting more.

"Sinister Peak," I growl, circling the white patch near its north face. He grins. I'm being dramatic. He plays along, growls too.

"Chickamin," I add for the mountain's glacier. He giggles at the name. It's goofy.

"Chickamin," he says, bobbing his head, which makes me laugh. I need to laugh. And in my mind I grab hold of him, though of course he doesn't know it, doesn't know this man is nearly falling. I'm squeezing him and digging in my always-trimmed fingernails, my pale hands, my polished boots. I'm hanging on, kid, I want to say. Tell me you have a rope, a plan. All I've got is this shiny gold badge, a buzz cut, a thinning hairline.

"Chickamin, Chickamin," he bobs his head, turning toward his parents, now behind him. He points to the glacier with the goofy name—Chinook Jargon for "metal."

We crowd in, we adults, unsettled, as a call sign comes across the radio. "One two fox trot en route to Marblemount."

"SAR talk," I say. "Ranger lingo." The boy looks up again, smiling.

And I think about those climbers at eight thousand feet, a thirtysomething man and his young girlfriend. I think about their ledge in the snow-soaked gray, how lost they must feel, how alarmed. "Idiots," some say, when they learn about these stories, as if every step you take is unforgivable. I think about a crest—one way or the other—and my own choices, my own regrets. Then my fellow rangers, packs on their backs, head out the door to the helipad.

"Chickamin," the boy says, loving the sound of it. His parents do too, as do I. Finally, we hear it: Tony setting down, his rotor wash drowning out the rain.

A RUCKSACK
RUMINATION

One of the generalities most often noted about Americans is that we are a restless, a dissatisfied, a searching people. We bridle and buck under failure, and we go mad with dissatisfaction in the face of success. We spend our time searching for security, and hate it when we get it.

—JOHN STEINBECK, *Paradox and Dream*

The spray paint surprised me. Neon orange. Unnatural. The slashes crisscrossed beneath my boots, contrasting with the emerging greenery crowding both sides of the trail. Chilled, I rezipped my collar. Scraps of clouds ascended the mountainside.

The paint marked the end for a fifty-four-year-old woman shot dead in that very spot the previous August. I'd forgotten about the incident, my mind on footfall in loose gravel, a much-needed break from the journey I'd been making from rural Rockport, through Seattle, to the tidal coves of Olympia on the southern tip of Puget Sound. And back up I-5 at week's end. I was seven months into a new job, a renegotiated marriage, a renegotiated identity unwedded to a dank river valley deep in the North Cascades. I had the same share of the mortgage, but also rent. I had a 320-mile round-trip commute and a futon in some lady's outbuilding, a studio her ex-husband, a psychologist, had used for appointments. It figures I would end up there. I remember the towering Douglas firs that swayed above the studio's roof, how windblown cones would plunk the metal as I lay awake, exhausted. I remember weeknight after weeknight, alone.

I'd been hired by The Evergreen State College to help Dr. Nalini Nadkarni, a world-renowned forest ecologist, launch the Sustainability in Prisons Project. Gathering dozens of collaborators, we took science and nature into the state's correctional system: green-collar job training, inmate-led research projects, and initiatives to save tax dollars as well as natural resources, from composting and recycling, to gardening and beekeeping, to refurbishing old bicycles and rehabilitating troubled dogs. Nalini wore mismatched socks—different colors and patterns—and on the morning I worked up the courage to ask why, when we were preparing to present to a state legislative committee, she replied with her typical zest. "Chaos theory, Jeff! Who knows what might happen next?"

Next. I was worn out by next. But there I was, back in Rockport, hiking up a subalpine meadow I could see from my half-a-house, my thighs starting to burn and my shoulders at last loosening from highway-weary weekdays that were anything but sustainable. Paula was working that day at the

Park Service visitor center, striving for a promotion as the district interpreter, a better-paid GS-11 position she was trying to land after serving a decade as a GS-9 ranger. My plan was to venture up 5,500-foot Sauk Mountain, where a fire lookout had once sat. The Beat poet Philip Whalen stood watch on Sauk in 1953, the same season his friend from Reed College, Gary Snyder, had been posted on Sourdough, thirty miles up the Skagit River. Fifty-six summers later, I was the one who was beat, from commuting, from renegotiating, and far from the beatitude Jack Kerouac had longed for in *On the Road*. But I hoped to spend a few hours with the poets and writers who had lured me to the mountains in the first place, at least my notion of them, as if wandering was simply something I could lay down in my journal, something I could look back on to appraise my life, to measure it. I could turn the chaos into story, a book perhaps, and maybe it would all be worth it—the stress, the journey, the countless decisions that seemed so random at the time but actually were leading somewhere, wherever I needed to go. Such as Sauk Mountain, a few days before my fortieth birthday.

But in that moment, I was lost. I'd wandered all that way, half a lifetime, thousands of miles from one job to the next, one bed to another, yet felt no closer to figuring out who I was or what I wanted, what I needed to feel contented. And committed—a committed husband. Or rather, settled, unplagued by indecision and the desire to renegotiate the terms of where Paula and I would live, and what we were living for. Instead, I felt imprisoned. Imprisoned by my own tendency to flee.

Then I stepped on that spray paint, the remnants of a forensic analysis. Four switchbacks up the trail, I encountered a second set of neon orange lines and an arrow pointing downhill, indicating where the shooter had stood to fire his gun. It all came rushing back: "the accident." Everybody called it that, though it led to a conviction of second-degree manslaughter. A fourteen-year-old hunter had pulled his trigger when he thought he saw a black bear rustling in the vegetation below, the wind-whipped fog obscuring his view. But it had only been a hiker leaning over her pack, perhaps stowing her jacket or grabbing a field guide to study a few plants. The woman was a longtime nature lover from the next valley over, the Stillaguamish. The boy was a Skagit kid, hunting legally on a Forest Service trail signed for "extra heavy" use. His grandfather had dropped him off with his older brother, another teenager, thinking that the morning's clouds would keep hikers away.

"Both families lost a life that day," I recall a neighbor saying, someone who'd lived in Rockport for decades and knew the boy's parents through the school system. I nodded in agreement, not wanting to offend with an opinion about guns—guns in the hands of teenagers.

At the time of the killing, early August 2008, bear season underway, Sauk's meadows would've radiated with wildflowers: lavender lupine, flame-red columbine, valerian, bright white, shoulder high, drunk on sunshine and snowmelt. But on *this* hike—June 20, 2009, according to my journal—only ground-hugging glacier lilies were blossoming, their petals creamy yellow, a shade that looks exactly like they taste, like sweet corn. I wrote that I put one in my mouth and thought about the black bears, how they rise from lowlands come summer to feast on blooms and bulbs and berries. I thought about the dead woman and the friend who'd been hiking with her, how she lay terrified, fearing another shot.

I suppose I felt fear too. Fear of how Sauk Mountain was no longer what it once was, at least for me. The wildflowers had become blood, the trees ghosts, the hike itself switchbacking to a loneliness I couldn't bear to imagine.

The thing is, more than a decade later, I still can't make sense of that time. My mind races with memories: an ironing board I bent violently during an argument in our second bedroom; thousands of haloing headlights, smeared through my windshield; men in red "DOC" shirts raising endangered Oregon spotted frogs; a female inmate, incarcerated for life, calmly taking notes like a scientist; and Nalini's laughter, her muscular arms, her tree-climbing equipment in my office in an Evergreen biology lab. In the years that followed, long after I worked for Nalini, whom *National Geographic* once called "Queen of the Forest Canopy," she nearly died from a fifty-foot freefall while conducting treetop research. Four surgeries later, after a coma, after weeks of hospital care and months and months of physical therapy, she continues to teach about her personal experience through lectures and papers on "disturbance, recovery, and resilience," much in the way ecosystems regenerate after a traumatic event.

Next. The science of next.

It would have been helpful to realize that at the time. It would be helpful to fully grasp it now, to embody it. But I'm not as durable as Nalini, nor as strong as that hiker's friend, who survived the hunting accident by lying in the wildflowers, their kaleidoscope of blooms providing unexpected camouflage. I imagine her rising to her feet, shell-shocked.

But I do recall sitting on Sauk's summit, taking in its 360-degree view for what would be my last time. The Skagit River swept back and forth in a widening valley, heading soundward, as I would the next evening. I dug into my rucksack to pull out my journal and then a small book, Philip Whalen's *The Diamond Noodle*, which I hadn't read since my own job upriver, in the national park. And for some reason—a decision that continues to elude me—I wrote down its first line: "The sun itself hadn't come up yet, but its light boiled up above the mountains."

I remember that light, that light before everything changes, the possibilities beyond daybreak, the promise. I remember hiking down, my boots gnawing through the gravel. Yellow glacier lilies. Orange spray paint. Scraps of clouds.

ONE MIGHTY YANK

I felt a rush of trust—felt that life might be not just
tolerable but beautiful, if I could only remember to find
the bare Present.

—DAVID JAMES DUNCAN, *River Teeth*

"Everybody loves turtles," Captain Eric would announce,
one hand on the mike, the other on the helm. I smiled
each time he said it, whenever we entered Broken Arrow
Slough, a haven for sun-loving reptiles. In that sinuous side
channel near La Crosse, a stretch of water would unfold like
clockwork. A passenger called out. Others started pointing.
Then we all saw sunbathers on logs: map turtles stacked like
leaning dominoes, tiny painteds with yellow-striped necks,
and softshells sprawling like wet leather pillows, their olive
carapaces gleaming and smooth. Adults flocked to the boat's
open windows. Kids jockeyed for a view from the front deck.
And as our pontoons tilted from all the excitement, I'd hand
the microphone to Eric, a proud father introducing his
children. "Everybody loves turtles," he'd say every time, as if
his own hand had placed each one of them on its slender perch
crowded with kin. "Warm days like this, there's more than we
can count, so keep your eyes peeled along the waterline."

For three summers, after Paula and I left the Pacific Northwest, I worked with Captain Eric on the Upper Mississippi River. Or as locals call it, the Upper Miss. Born and raised in Wisconsin, Eric was four years younger than me, and much bigger, with a sunburned face and an ornery cowlick, which made his straight blond hair look perpetually windblown. His accent was nasally, his wit sharp, and his résumé included far more than being a tour boat captain. As a young man in the Navy, he'd served as a submarine technician who knew every inch of the vessel blindfolded, in case of blackouts. He'd since earned his master's degree in marketing, fathered two sons, and was married to a religion professor at the Catholic university in town. And he could fix anything on our boat—its dual engines, its leaky roof, its stinky head. In fact, he dreamed of purchasing it from our boss, Captain Jack, a retired towboat captain downriver in Prairie du Chien, though when Jack died of cancer, his widow had other plans for the company. "I've got ideas," Eric would say. "Lots of ideas."

Our specialty? Ecotours. Forty-passenger cruises destined for the backwaters, which were miles wide only minutes from our dock. We loved our tagline: "Explore more! See more!" Twenty bucks a head, alcohol allowed. This was La Crosse, after all. This was Wisconsin. This was the adventure not of Lewis and Clark heading westward, but of Zebulon Pike in 1805, sent by President Thomas Jefferson up the Mississippi toward Canada. Northward. Zebward!

As the onboard naturalist, binoculars at the ready, I knew my job was more than passing out skulls and skins and hands-on props, and acting as the first mate for docking and passenger safety. I'd also been hired to laugh. To laugh at Eric's jokes. I was his sidekick, to be sure, which I embraced because the Upper Miss had stolen my heart. Rivers do that, you know. They pull your wildest organ right out of your chest and infuse it with ten thousand creeks. Before long, herons and bluegills and mayflies start feeling like extended family. You learn where to spot an eagle on a snag or a muskrat shouldering the bank, and you're thrilled when someone smiles alongside you like a toddler stalking her first frog. Watching wildlife feels good—it's that simple. I'd see a pelican skimming a sandbar, and my spirit was bound to soar with it. I'd dip my net into soupy shallows, and grabbing my bucket was all that mattered. It brimmed, like me, with creekjoy.

Eric didn't know it, but I needed him. Not only the job, but him. During our years living along the Upper Miss, I needed to work on a boat, needed to say, "Cap'n," needed to participate in the jokes and banter and fish-tale stories about nature and people and our restroom. "That's not just a door that opens to the river!" Eric would welcome our guests, pointing at the head. If they laughed, he'd wink at me. If they didn't, he'd shrug.

Looking back, I'm not sure what the feeling was—camaraderie, brotherly affection? What was that rush of little-boy excitement compelling me to make up silly words? All I know is I felt reborn each time I descended the aluminum gangway leading to our dock: *clomp, clomp, creekjoy.* There is something intensely gratifying, even nourishing, about stepping onto whatever level an indomitable waterway happens to be in that hour, whether it's rising with the runoff of upstream storms, or of snowmelt, or from the spring thaw of an immeasurable layer cake of frozen soil, or when it's falling, falling, falling, summer worn, destined for drought. Rivers remind us that the world is bigger than us, our worries, our griefs. It's bigger. It's stronger. It will carry us along to new territory.

Certainly, clomping down the gangway my first time, I understood I was born fewer than five hundred miles from La Crosse, in central Indiana, which made me a native of the vast Mississippi watershed, specifically Buck Creek, which feeds Sugar Creek, which feeds the White River, which feeds the Wabash, which feeds the Ohio, all bound for the Big Muddy. But I was not a native of the *Upper* Midwest. And prior to settling in Wisconsin, home had been the Pacific-leaning slope of the North Cascades, lifeblood of the Skagit River. Paula and I had moved to La Crosse for her job with a new agency, after she had decided to sue the Park Service, her employer for more than two decades. It would be a sullen, secretive, paranoid fresh start. Our dreams had dried up. Our marriage nearly had.

One lonely winter's week, we'd driven across the pale, brittle hues of the American West, the topography flattening each mile eastward, and had descended Minnesota's bluffs to traverse snow-white sloughs and skeletal, leafless islands. The sunsets behind us had been as pink as salmon, creatures we'd cherished as Northwesterners. For years we'd lived along a whitewater stream racing to balmy Puget Sound. But looking across the frozen Upper Miss, its ice dotted with anglers and four-by-fours, we'd wondered how anyone could survive in that place, its January's bone-chilling cold. Yet the harsh weather faded quickly that year—no snow even in March—and soon we were lulled out of doors as migrating birds returned in waves. One day it was sandhills, next it was warblers, then came autumn and all the tundra swans, their honking a boisterous song from the Arctic: "Onward! Onward! Onward!"

We were carried along, I see now, by the river, the birds, each other.

"To hope is to give yourself to the future," Rebecca Solnit wrote, "and that commitment to the future makes the present inhabitable." I agree. And yet I don't.

That sounds like something Captain Eric and I would debate in the quiet moments between tours, when we'd cut the jokes and bond over heartfelt words, words devoted to exactly that: whether we were merely savoring the present through Huck Finn forays, through meanderings, through eagle spotting and macroinvertebrate sorting, or if we actually had a plan for the future, a plan each of us could call a career. I'd tell him about my circuitous past, my mistakes and misgivings, my struggle to reinvent myself after management jobs and ranger jobs, plus my work at the time on a second master's degree—creative writing, which seemed to be in those moments (and in this sentence even now) the most useless degree anyone could pursue in order to better his employment. And Eric would talk about his own dreams, his own woes, surprising me with lines like "I would've been fine not having kids." "Singapore, what a cool place." Or "When it comes down to it, I might be an atheist."

Man, I loved that guy. His ideas. Lots of ideas.

And don't forget his strength. One time on the waterfront, near our dock beside the levee, as the Upper Miss muscled along in its surly, opaque channel, a tourist fell into the water. He panicked and soon weakened. As he clung to the dock, his feet flailing downstream, Eric leaned over the edge and with one hand, one mighty yank, lifted the man to safety. It took all of sixty seconds for the scene to play out—the lifesaving, the slopslush sound of the saving—and in typical Wisconsin fashion, there were no cheers or hugs or long speeches afterward, only a big man doing big-man things. Followed by jokes.

Or so I heard; I wasn't at work that day. Michelle, a part-time student and full-time mom who often covered my days off, told me about the incident, and I believed her. I believed every word. Eric inspired her as well, entertained her, saved her, and together we'd save our captain through the nonstop schedule of warmer months. We'd laugh with him, pass the microphone, and fill our buckets in the backwaters. It may not have been the best job I've had, but the best coworkers, you betcha.

Sure enough, when I started teaching as an adjunct at the University of Wisconsin-La Crosse, seldom did I converse with a professor and hear what Eric had offered: curiosity, modesty, and empathy. A sense of humor. A joke. My colleagues on campus, by comparison, seemed cynical, at times backbiting. To pursue a PhD felt pointless. Tenure? What a drag. But whenever I stepped out of my classroom, taking a weekend shift on the river, I became a little boy all over again. Clomp, clomp, hope.

What a tricky word *hope* is, so prone to typos. Change *h* to *n*, you've got a letdown, *p* to *l*, a reminder: stop digging, or deeper and deeper you go. Thank goodness for Eric, one mighty Yank. Thank goodness for turtles. Thank goodness for the birds that saved my wife, heading Zebward, Zebward, Zebward.

WAITING FOR RAIN

The popular view of Appalachia is a land where every man is willing, at the drop of a proverbial overall strap, to shoot, fight, or fuck anything on hind legs. We're men who buy half-pints of boot-legged liquor and throw the lids away in order to finish the whiskey in one laughing, brawling night, not caring where we wake or how far from home. Men alleged to eat spiders off the floor to display our strength, a downright ornery bunch.

The dirt truth is a hair different.

—CHRIS OFFUTT, *The Same River Twice*

In the wrinkled hardwood hills of southern Kentucky, near the Cumberland River's lazy meander into Tennessee, Paula and I turned off Highway 90 three miles east of Willow Shade. It was mid-September 2010, the end of a searing, drought-weary summer, and nearly three decades since my last visit. I was forty-one, Paula forty-five, and we'd recently moved to Wisconsin from out west. Driving down to Kentucky was part of rooting ourselves, a week to explore the center of the country, where I grew up, and to hike in a few parks such as Mammoth Cave. We'd also wanted to visit my father's grave, located nearby in Beaumont. Here, along this dead end, was his birthplace.

I eased our Subaru up the shallow valley, lowering my window to listen. Crows cawed in the windless treetops. A blue jay chattered nearby. A sun-bleached barn sat in an empty field where tobacco plants once grew over my head, their huge green leaves crowding a gravel lane. Today the paved road was silent, leaving only a memory to fill my ears: the sound of Dad's '73 Chevy Impala, its fenders pinging with ricochets.

We continued driving with our windows down, the air smelling of dust and goldenrod and seed-heavy grasses leaning over the pavement. Hickories and oaks lined the low-slung ridges. The sky was a cloudless haze.

"Is that it?" Paula asked, looking to our left. A thin brownish pool inched by.

"Yes," I said, "I think so," recalling my soaked jeans as a kid. I imagined the waterway in early summer, flowing fast and full over pale shale stones. Now, however, it hardly looked like a stream, more like a drainage ditch than a habitat. It was the dry season, I knew, but I was still disappointed. I had hoped to walk through its riffles.

We paused beside a small, dilapidated, cream-colored house amid scraggly saplings and weedy grass. The porch brimmed with old tools and assorted plastic bottles, a navy blue recliner, a cabinet with a sink. The windows were murky, the curtains drawn. The place looked abandoned long ago.

"Aunt Ruby," I said, snapping a photo, "was always sitting right there."

Idling, I described my great-aunt, her salt-and-pepper hair, thick calves, and rough hands, how she sat on a couch on that drooping front porch, waving a fan to cool herself. Her hugs smelled like bacon as she called me "punkin," her twangy accent both frightening and fascinating. Back then I had no idea how old she was, and now I'd forgotten her last name. But I did remember she was Dad's favorite aunt—a mirror image of his father's round face. She's kin, Dad would say, good people, phrases I rarely heard up north.

The creek trickled behind the house beneath low-hanging maples and through a concrete culvert that looked out of place. "That's where I'd walk down to the water, just a tractor path, a few stones to hop across." I recounted a tall, skinny, red and white barn with smoke seeping through its walls and pooling in the air. A farmer had lit small fires on the barn's dirt floor to dry out the tobacco hanging from the rafters. "Makes it taste good," Dad once told me as he puffed on a cigarette. Probably a Winston, his favorite brand.

The image lingered with us as Paula and I drove to a fork in the pavement with two green street signs. One route followed Pitman Creek toward its source in the hills, perhaps two or three miles away. Veering right followed Shaw Creek, a tributary to Pitman, and that way was marked with my family name. "MUSE RD," the sign read in white capital letters, and I felt pride, curiosity, regret. I felt emotions a man feels, I suppose.

Pitman Creek, Muse Road, my long-dead father—all of them flowed through me in that moment. We'd driven hundreds of miles south after looking at satellite photos, scrolling closer and closer on our computer. "Dad was born here," I'd said as we surveyed Google Maps from our home along the Upper Mississippi River. Tracing the topography with my finger, I'd read aloud the place names, Kentucky a mirage, yet vivid. "It was the wildest place I knew as a boy—thunderstorms, caves, hollows. I hunted crawdads in this stream by pulling up flat rocks, then catching them in a coffee can pierced with nail holes."

Now, almost thirty years later, I was staring at that road sign with my name on it. The Muses were my kin and this was my father's birthplace, but, really, what had lured us this far south? I let off the brake to head upstream. I needed to retrace my path and share it with Paula. And to be honest, I was looking for more than Dad. That afternoon, up Muse Road, I sought answers.

"We tell ourselves stories in order to live," wrote Joan Didion, whose essays explore the nature of truth telling. What actually happened, she might ask, and what's interpretation? Is recollection just remaking the past?

My mother says I've told stories all my life, mixing what occurred with what I made up. These days I'm unsure of the stories I tell myself, especially when my father is a main character. I may be casting him as a rural hero, though growing up, I viewed him as the town fool. Where did the embarrassment go? Did this change of heart come when he died at fifty-four, or sooner when I'd walked a few steps in his shoes? Maybe all I'm doing is remaking him, turning the father I had into the one I wanted.

The thing is, if you had asked me to describe him in my late teens, I likely would've muttered the bare minimum. "He lives in Indianapolis, works at Chrysler, and divorced my mother when I was eight." But inside my head I would've ranted with resentment: Dad's always been a drinker, a drunk. He hangs out at the Honky Tonk Tavern on Brookside Avenue. He wears headbands, cutoff jeans, flip-flop sandals, and says, "Look at them 'maters" in his city lot. He owns a duplex with his chain-smoking mom next door, and keeps Papa Shaw's Chevy pickup in his garage. He's got two rototillers, three lawnmowers, who knows what else out there. He's always buying tools, making deals, paying cash. And he likes to tell dirty jokes to his union buddies, guys like Big Bob and a stroke-impaired hard drinker named Tim. They met years ago at the Chrysler plant on Indy's east side, though since it closed, Dad commutes to the transmission factory in Kokomo. Now he stays weeknights in a trailer up there. A second girlfriend, more buddies, more drinking.

"If you're going to spend time with Dad," my brother, Alan, once warned me, "drive your own car so you don't get trapped." He understood stopping by was like Russian roulette; you never knew how uncomfortable you'd get. Crass humor, foul language, the stench of cigarettes. Friends who wandered in and dozed off. Everyone hung out with our father, I learned early on. Having his sons around did nothing to slow the party.

Even worse were the times when Dad was alone, when our conversations turned toward his regrets. "Your mom is an amazing lady," he'd repeat, jangling the ice cubes in his glass of rum and coke. "You better treat her with respect . . . she deserves respect. I blew it, that's for sure. I fucking blew it."

Along Muse Road, Paula and I parked about a half mile up the valley, where I walked toward an older man working beside a mobile home. He wore a white T-shirt, a silver wristwatch, and a ball cap with a corporate logo. He'd been hammering on a rusty plow in the back of his driveway. "I'm James Whitlow," he said, and I recognized his face while shaking his hand. We'd met at Dad's funeral in 1998, though I'd forgotten his name in the twelve years since.

"Ruby was my mother," he explained. "I'm your cousin. Been here all my life." As I shook his hand again, I motioned for Paula to join us, and we all settled into a picnic table under a shade tree.

James had recently helped his longtime employer, Dana Corporation, relocate its auto parts factory from Glasgow, Kentucky, to central Mexico. He said, "Your Uncle Stanley," Dad's brother, "also worked there, until cancer took him from us a while back." He talked candidly about his troubles as if we'd always known him, saying he got laid off but had learned a little Spanish along the way. "I spent a couple months training Mexicans to take my job. They were so thankful, so happy for the work, it made it easier."

James said he stayed in a city of three million people, visited Acapulco, and met policemen fighting drug cartels. Paula followed his tale with rapt interest, having visited Mexico several times to attend language schools. I paid attention the best that I could, but my mind filled with questions, with remorse: How had I not remembered that James lived up Shaw Creek, or that Whitlow was Aunt Ruby's married name? And why hadn't I gone to Uncle Stanley's funeral? Where was I? Was I getting along with Dad? The questions weren't the kind to share aloud. Instead I focused on my cousin's face, his voice.

As I listened to James begin talking about my father, how they were born only six years apart, I was mesmerized by his vowel-heavy accent, the way his words fell together so melodically. "If you want to" came out "yunt to" as he suggested where to look around. "Up there" was "up air" when he pointed to a hillside. And the word "holler" I remembered hearing as a boy: a wooded valley as narrow as cupped hands.

"Keith and I used to go squirrel hunting when he'd come down on weekends," James said. "He'd drive up with a trunk full of beer, grinning from ear to ear." Paula and I laughed at the animation of his storytelling, his hands mimicking a pull tab, then tossing it aside.

Don't get me wrong—James Whitlow is a smart man. Travels, knows business, follows the news. When I introduced him to Paula, he was charming and attentive, and I admired his yes-sirs, his no-ma'ams. Yet I was spellbound by his features and mannerisms, how his speech unearthed another era. I could hear the curl of Dad's tongue in his voice and found myself twanging a bit as well. "I'm taking my wife for a stroll down memory lane," I said, "trying to relive my childhood a long, long time ago." James nodded with pleasure, as did Dora, his wife, who had joined us from inside the mobile home.

Paula looked enthralled as we all spoke affectionately, as if she were finally seeing my father in person. Like her, I felt a surprising sensation, swelling, tingling, leaking out.

"Not much has changed here," I said, looking down. My face blushed. My eyes watered, blurred.

"Road's paved," James said, thumbing over his shoulder. "And they're logging on the hill over yonder." But nobody grew tobacco anymore, he said. Mostly cows now, a few horses behind barbed wire. Still, people hunted upstream—the state forest land I'd seen on our map.

As we grew more comfortable, James spoke in a serious tone. "You know, Jeff, I always looked up to your father." Dora rocked in her seat, nodding in agreement. "But even when he was young, he was quite a drinker, Keith was. At twelve or thirteen, he had to have his stomach pumped. A bunch of older boys left him passed out on the porch."

I thought of my early road trips with Dad in the Impala, how he drank from a can or bottle wrapped in a paper bag. In my mind's eye, I could see it wedged between his legs. I could hear the bag crinkle as he tilted it.

"Keith had a heart of gold," Dora said emphatically, changing the subject by speaking kindly of my father. "He had a way of checking on everybody, asking if they needed any help." She trailed on, mentioning names I didn't know.

I said he'd done the same for his friends back in Indianapolis, including a quiet man named Jack, who'd moved in with Dad a year or two before his death. I also thought of Dad's house when I visited as a teenager—the cigarette smoke, the raspy voices, the dirty jokes.

"You're right," I said. "He was a good man." And I missed him, sitting at that picnic table. We all did.

It's difficult to sort out these feelings I have for my father, the way cigarette smoke or someone's beer-soured breath can conjure him in my senses, in my heart, in unpredictably complicated ways. On one hand, such moments lead to nostalgia, but on the other, confusion, a reluctant longing. I'll remember the times he leaned over to kiss me goodbye, his black mustache scraping my forehead like tiny bristles, a fleshy sensation that lingered in the long minutes after he was gone, after he had crossed the door's threshold and driven away. Or I'll remember years later when I was becoming a man myself, much bigger and taller than him, when he was sitting in his own living room or on his front porch in Indianapolis, drinking from that sweaty glass of rum and coke, its bottom dripping onto a glass end table flecked with ashes and tree pollen and the dust of city streets, and again I'd feel his mustache against my skin—grayer now, thinner, but still prickly, still leaving a mark that lingered as *I* drove away.

Before departing, though, passing through his front gate, I'd hear him whistle and call out, "Hey, boy! Don't let your meat loaf!" Or some such nonsense. Even Dad's goodbyes could be a joke—funny, clever, but always crass. And troubling in a way I couldn't figure out. It's complicated, as I said. Confusing.

Or am I imagining all of this, not only what happened but also how it made me feel, how it still makes me feel as a grown man, three years shy of Dad's age when he died? Truth is, I was deeply ashamed during my teenage years, including by his hillbilly first name, Wendell. At least that's what I thought a hillbilly sounded like: Wendell Muse from Dubre, Kentucky. The backwoods. The sticks! Thank goodness, most people called him Keith, his middle name. Wendell was a hick, a hayseed, or, as Dad liked to call himself, a redneck. Obviously, anything I called him sounded like disappointment, if not anger or gut-gnawing dread. I hated holidays, the drunk phone calls, his excuses for being late— that is, if he showed up at all. I first felt it after the divorce when I was eight, when I'd see the bag-wrapped bottle on our drives to Dairy Queen. An hour or two, tops, that was our relationship. That and a few road trips to Kentucky. Yet how can a child ever come to know his father over a Brazier burger and butterscotch malt? The scrape of Dad's mustache was surely real. All the rest? Elusive.

I guess these memories are all that's left when a son wants to forgive, or needs to, but even forgiveness has its own kind of compromise, a remaking of the people involved. Didion was right: I'm telling this story in order to live. To live with myself and with Dad.

By my late twenties, though, not long before he died, my feelings had actually changed for the better, for reasons that only now make any sense. Empathy had crept into my heart, and I had simply stopped having any expectations. Peer pressure was a thing of the past; I cared less and less about what people thought. And by then I had my own track record as a man, having moved away after college and come home browbeaten. I'd experienced dead-end jobs and busted relationships. I'd earned little money and had school loans, debt. And on both coasts I'd struggled to hang on to happiness, watching women walk away exhausted, exhausted with me. Maybe Muse men are all alike, I'd begun to think. Bound to struggle, fail, disappoint.

I didn't drink back then, and seldom do now. I've always feared alcohol—and heredity. But is drinking what troubles me? Is it abandonment? Is forgiveness the wrong word, the wrong intention? Instead, I want to understand him. I want to know him better, and perhaps myself. Maybe that's what lured Paula and me from Wisconsin, lured us down the Mississippi, east to Kentucky. My father was born in that little valley. Was I?

Cumberland County is poor. Poor, rugged, and isolated. It sits on a westward-leaning plateau—shale, sandstone, limestone, every inch shaped by water. In 2010 the population was 6,856, half of its 1940s heyday. Roughly a quarter of its residents lived below the US poverty line, about $11,000 per year. The biggest town in the county is Burkesville, established on the Cumberland River in 1846. Not long after that, during the Civil War, soldiers fought along its banks, wearing blue or gray.

After the war, in 1867, John Muir passed through. Traveling from Indiana to Florida, the future Sierra Club president and advocate for national parks planned to walk "by the wildest, leafiest, and least trodden way I could find." On September 8, near what would become my father's birthplace, Muir described a "deep, green, bossy sea of waving, flowing hilltops." Today, Kentucky Route 90 is the John Muir Highway.

To reach the community of Dubre from the Cumberland River, you have to travel ten miles up Marrowbone Creek, heading northwest from Burkesville. It's a slow climb through iron-rich layers—an ancient seabed, bisected. My great-grandfather, Bedford Muse, who descended from John Muse Sr., the first Muse to emigrate from England to Virginia in the seventeenth century, may have taken this route. By the early 1900s, he'd cleared a patch of floodplain forest to farm tobacco. Bedford and his wife, Cenia, went on to have nine children, including Victor, my dad's father, born in 1920. When "Vic" married Hazel Shaw, who would become my grandmother, they moved into a shack about a quarter mile downstream. That's where my father was born in 1943, among many cousins with surnames from the British Isles.

Dad once showed me the house in the midseventies, though by then only mice and snakes skittered inside. I remember the decaying floorboards and newsprint wallpaper. I remember a hornet's nest, its swirls of gray. "Where did the kids sleep?" I asked, seeing only one bedroom. "The same mattress," Dad said, "all of us." Even now I can't help but wonder, was he pulling my leg? Dad teased everybody, teased and tickled.

Hazel would bear a girl and two more boys along Shaw Creek, though Welby, the son right after Dad, lived only one day. Then Vic took his family north to find work in Indianapolis, where my youngest uncle was born fifteen years after my father. If my math is correct, they left Dubre in 1957, after Dad had completed the eighth grade in Burkesville— the extent of his education. Dad said he worked in a battery factory instead of going to high school. He chased pretty girls like my mom and drank beer with his buddies. Store-bought alcohol had been scarce back in southern Kentucky; Cumberland remained a dry county until 2016. But thanks to moonshine, Dad told me, he learned how to hold his liquor. He learned how to handle "the hard stuff," along with

Budweiser. Driving up Muse Road, I didn't expect to recall these memories. I didn't expect to meet James Whitlow, let alone swap stories.

Sitting at my cousin's picnic table, I described my recollections of Pitman Creek, how Dad and I would visit Aunt Ruby, then head upstream. "Along the way, he'd point at a shack, half hidden in summertime weeds, saying he was born there during World War II." Usually about that time, Dad would whistle at a man in a front yard. He'd park the car, laugh, light a cigarette. From what I recall, I never stuck around for their conversation, instead hurrying across the lane to investigate the stream. But standing in the water, I could still hear my father's voice. More cars pulled up. Men whistled. Men laughed.

I asked James if he remembered anything like this during one of our visits, if Dad and I had stopped by his place or nearby. "Sure," he said matter-of-factly, "you always did, you know that. I watched you play in that creek right there, catching crawdads."

I nodded in silence as my nose started tingling again, the memories like high water, a sudden flood. I imagined my soggy jeans, the dripping coffee can, the cool air. I imagined tiptoeing through the stream, searching for prey. Crayfish dart backward, leaving contrails of smoky dust. You must lift the stones delicately to keep the water clear. Steady now, I used to tell myself. Lift slowly, lower the can. Watch out for those claws. Steady, steady.

Paula's eyes teared up as she watched mine do the same. She knew I'd spent two decades working on rivers. But until talking to my cousin, I hadn't figured it out. I hadn't realized how my career had started. How my life had.

After college I'd been a camp counselor on Indiana's Flat Rock River and taught two seasons in New York aboard a Hudson River sailboat. I'd mapped wetlands in western Oregon and directed a learning center in Washington's Cascades, crossing a dam each day four hundred feet above whitewater. Even that summer in Wisconsin, our home for less than a year, I'd been teaching as a tour boat naturalist on the Upper Mississippi. In the backwaters I'd dip a net, occasionally catching a crawdad, which would wriggle in my muddy hand, then dart around my bucket. And though I'd always known that Kentucky is where I fell in love with nature, I hadn't given any credit to Dad, not a word of thanks. Yet if that roadside creek is where my journey began—my identity, not just my career—it was my father, Wendell Keith Muse, who'd set me afloat.

"Right there," James pointed. "Your dad and I watched you."

On the day before my father died in May 1998, a Saturday, I stood in a shallow, mud-bottomed stream northeast of Indianapolis, running a workshop for Hoosier Riverwatch, a citizen science program of the Department of Natural Resources. I'd been teaching schoolteachers and farmers and activists how to monitor creeks throughout Indiana—where I grew up, where I come from, and the place I've left behind on more than one occasion. I drove a white panel van with a decal of an adult mayfly on each side, its long tail curling toward the sky like a fly-fishing rod, always casting, casting, casting. I loved that image, loved how it made me feel—part scientist, part explorer, a professional in hip boots.

Scientists call the order of mayflies Ephemeroptera, Latin for "short-lived wing," and though there are two thousand species worldwide, they all have one thing in common: each dies quickly after emerging from the water. During their aquatic stages over many months, they metamorphose from egg to nymph, eventually "hatching" as flying adults without functional mouths. At that point, instead of eating, they focus on finding a mate, ensuring their fertilized eggs fall back into the water. Some species get a day or two to pass on their genes, others a few hours, or only minutes.

My workshop took place in Anderson, Indiana, a town still reeling from the closure of its General Motors plant, reminding me of the decades Dad had worked for Chrysler, building cars through boom and bust. That afternoon he was an hour north in Kokomo, returning to his trailer after a surgery several days earlier. A polyp-filled segment of his colon had been removed, and the pain, he'd said in his hospital bed, was "godawful."

When Alan and I visited him after the operation, Dad was agitated, hardly himself. A row of staples pierced his stomach.

He trembled with craving. "I can come by on Sunday," I told him, "to buy groceries, whatever you need." Dad said a neighbor he called Dino would give him a ride home. "I can bring some things from my job," I said, "samples of aquatic insects—mayflies and other critters from all over the state."

"Sure, son," my father grimaced. "Bring your bugs."

On Saturday night, when he was back in his trailer, I called Dad to remind him of my visit. He was still irritable. His pain pills weren't helping. "The Pacers are in the playoffs," I said. "They're playing Michael Jordan and the Bulls. You like basketball? Want to watch the game?"

All he did was grumble, mentioning Dino, the neighbor I hadn't met. "He'll give me a ride," Dad said. "The market's close." I got angry, raising my voice, telling him to stay put for the night, that I'd be there by nine the next day, ready to shop.

When we hung up the phone that evening, neither of us knew it would be our last conversation. It didn't even sound like my father. Cranky. Sober. And so when I arrived at his trailer on Sunday, later than I'd intended, his door was locked and he didn't answer when I knocked and knocked. I sat on his wooden stoop as the heat and humidity came on, and thought about watching that basketball game, how I deserved to relax. I was a child, I see now, thinking he'd failed me again, that he'd driven off with a buddy—another damn nickname. Why else would the door be locked? His place in Indianapolis was always open. I waited, brooding, as cars passed by. I knew nothing about Dino. The same bullshit, same as always. Dad's life was a mystery to me. Mystery and farce.

I left my business card in his doorframe, which now seems so arrogant, so callous. Like my DNR uniform, it made me feel important. I wrote a note on the back: "Where are you? Give me a call." Later, when I told my mother, she thought nothing of it. "Jeffrey," she said, "that's just the way he is."

Why didn't I worry when I heard nothing that afternoon? Why didn't I call *him*? Did I even care? I can think of dozens of possibilities, a lifetime of second-guessing, but all I know for certain is that it was habit. Dad's habit. My habit. The habit of our family. And as much as I hate saying it, losing him had never crossed my mind. I'd spent years dreading whenever we did talk on the phone. Liquored up, his drawl was raspier, more southern, more redneck. "Hey, youngin," he might say. "How's it hanging?"

Maybe I didn't call for that reason—the dread behind the habit. What I do remember, the only truth I know, is the Pacers lost. And I know that on Monday morning I was back in my cubicle at the State Capitol, wearing a tie and sport coat for a meeting with my boss. Then the phone on my desk started ringing—its red light blinking, blinking, blinking—and on the other end of the line was a sheriff's office. "Sir, an ambulance has been dispatched to your father's residence."

How strange, I thought, to hear such words and not know what a son should do, though the dispatcher told me that was all she could say, and to call the hospital. My coworkers could hear me dialing the phone, standing up, and raising my voice, then swearing at useless answers after desperate questions. "Has Keith Muse been admitted?" I asked. "No? Where the hell is he? The hospital's only a few miles from his goddamn trailer!" I slammed the receiver down, glancing at my cubicle's entry. Three men stood there watching me, all wearing ties.

After my third try with the emergency room, my light blinked with an incoming call. "Mr. Muse," a voice said, "I'm the Howard County coroner. I don't typically do this over the phone, but you deserve answers. I'm sorry to say, your father is dead."

Dad had died in his trailer from what appeared to be natural causes. The coroner said he'd passed away sometime the previous day. A neighbor had found him, he explained, by using a hide-a-key above the front door. "I'm calling you because I have your business card. When were you there?"

I told him it was later than I'd planned—"10:00 a.m., 10:30"—and that I'd sat on the stoop for a half hour, probably less. I drove my own car, I could've said. I wasn't trapped. I could leave. "Our relationship was . . ." My voice cracked. "It's hard to explain."

After thanking the coroner, I dialed the phone, reaching Alan, my big brother. "Dad's dead," I told him, stunned. "In his trailer." Alan didn't know how to react either—desperate questions, useless answers—but I explained what I could from the coroner, staring at my desk. Little jars of insects lined the wall, each with a specimen preserved in formaldehyde. The mayflies were my favorite—such long tails. I remembered how Dad had loved to fish, how he'd taken me as a boy to Kentucky. Bluegill, bass, crappie. We would fish all day.

Sometimes I feel like a thin creek, nearly empty, waiting for rain. Sometimes laughter feels forced. Sometimes life does. Sometimes I envy my dad, his silly jokes and all his buddies, the way he smiles in the photographs he left behind. Despite his mistakes as a father, I think of him fondly nowadays. He was a rousing ringleader of gravel-voiced men. And it's not unusual, I know, for an alcoholic's son to turn out jaded, if not a bit somber or stubbornly sober. I tend to expect the worst in most situations, preparing to rise above it, or to brace myself, knowing I'll survive. Then again, I'm like my father in the way I often cope with loss, though I retreat into wild places instead of beer. He drank. I wander. Shame is a territory, an internal landscape. We've both walked through it in our own way.

James Whitlow's kind face made me want to tell the whole story, to piece it together, not only how Dad had died but also the guilt I felt. And returning to Pitman and Shaw creeks, in which my father must've played as a boy, made me feel understanding and perhaps understood. I felt Dad's presence. I felt like I could talk to him.

A few days after his funeral, Alan and I cleaned out his trailer—the first time either of us had been inside. There were Budweiser cans on the coffee table. Get-well cards. A remote control. A skillet on the stove was layered with grease. Ashtrays overflowed. The black tennis shoes he wore on the assembly line sat next to his couch, side by side, evidence of his care and tidiness with tools and work clothes. But like the times I'd visited Dad as a boy, I held his belongings at an awkward distance, never knowing them intimately as I had my mother's. What do you call that sensation—part craving, part repulsion? Do other sons feel it? Do other men? I felt it especially in the cramped hallway, kneeling where Dad had died, lying on his back, where he'd fallen across the bathroom's threshold, his torso spilling outward. I pressed my hand in the bloody circle where his head had lain upright, and I looked at the dried vomit, spattered and sprawling. It appeared to trail from the toilet, to the white vinyl, to the gold carpet, turning from a nearly clear film to something brown. At that point Dad had been faceup only three feet from the outdoor stoop. All that separated us when I'd sat there was a flimsy door—a piece of shit, I'd thought, when I banged on it days earlier.

Did my father die while I brooded there, or could I have saved him had I shown up sooner? The doctor who performed the autopsy said, "Not likely." The surgical wounds in Dad's abdomen hadn't ruptured from his intense vomiting, nor had he asphyxiated, throwing up on his back. Instead, the doctor said, arrhythmia was the cause of death. His heart broke from an irregular beat—that's how I took it. As for what caused the arrhythmia, that's the habit, or addiction: Dad died with a blood alcohol level of 0.18. "Fatal," the doctor said, "when you're taking pain meds."

I wanted to share all of this with James as we stood along Muse Road, but when I worked up the courage to explain it, a logging truck eased by. Its diesel engine drowned out our conversation, the exhaust blurring the September sky, which made the scenery look like a mirage, I thought, or maybe a sign. Was it time to let things lie, to lighten up? Besides, James's cell phone had been ringing; neighbors had seen our car. "Keith Muse's boy," he'd answered. "Jeff, his youngest." When one of them pulled up, I was intrigued by the four-wheeler he sat on. It was outfitted with a rifle, a fishing pole, and a little red cooler.

The man's name was Odie Turner. He stopped by for only a few minutes. "I'm heading up the creek," he said, "to hunt with my son." Again, handshakes made their rounds, we talked about our travels, our journey, and Odie said he'd always lived nearby, that he'd grown up with Dad. Yet he didn't say much more than that—he seemed shy but entirely at ease—though by then I was spent emotionally and pleased to stand still. I smiled at Odie warmly. He smiled back in a sleeveless tee. He was muscular. His hair was gray, as was his mustache.

"What's that?" Paula asked, pointing at the four-wheeler's handlebars. A golf club was turned upside down, fastened vertically with duct tape.

"Spiderweb catcher," Odie said, squinting while ducking his head. He winked at Paula, flirting, the way Dad would have.

I chuckled but kept staring. My gaze was fixed on Odie. His tan, thick arms. The lines on his face. He was my father reincarnated, how his teasing came so naturally, and when he rode off minutes later, I wanted to go with him. The four-wheeler disappeared through the trees, echoing up Shaw Creek, leaving dust to settle around us, along with silence.

"Cousin," I said to James, "we best be going." Paula's hand reached for mine, and I held on tight.

After we said goodbye to James and Dora and turned west on Highway 90, Paula and I stopped by the Beaumont cemetery to visit Dad's grave. Grandma Hazel lay to one side, her site newer, its grass sparse, and to the other lay tiny Welby and Grandpa Vic. I thought about the week of Dad's death, the shock, the regret, how Alan and I had created a time capsule when we filled his casket. We dressed him in a dark gray suit based on a picture from my college graduation, and around his arms and shoulders set everyday things. Cutoff jeans. A headband—his favorite, red, white, and blue. And three ball caps with dirty jokes on the front, all gifts from his friends. In the coffin's drawer above Dad's waist, I slid an envelope with a crushed beer can, with a note expressing forgiveness and asking for it. We set more, much more inside, as if trying to make him feel at home. Winstons, toothpicks, nail clippers, things he always carried. And before putting him in the ground, we encircled his tombstone with an epigraph: "Father. Son. Brother. Friend."

I don't know if we did the right thing, stuffing his casket with so many items, trying to replace years of awkwardness with appreciation. But standing at Dad's grave with Paula, knowing he lay below us, I wanted to squeeze something else inside, something serious. If I could've given him a shard of shale, a flat stone from a crawdad creek, I would've felt certain he knew that I did love him. That I love him still. That I understand. I understand now all men are flawed.

On the other hand, if I know my father, he would've preferred something lighthearted. Odie's spiderweb catcher, for instance. Better yet, Odie's cooler. I imagine Dad laughing at the prospect, cracking jokes, teasing us all. Maybe the drinking made him like that. I no longer care. I only wish I could pick up the phone and hear his voice.

Yet I know this story can't end on forgiveness, or longing, even love. It's about more than that, I've come to learn. Always has been. It's about truth, elusive truth, including my own flaws. I first wrote this at forty-four, after three years of fits and starts. Three years of looking at photographs. Three years of maps. Three more years of working on rivers, in the Mississippi's muddy backwaters—hundreds of cruises on a tour boat, my hands always wet. I wish I could've said it was a "dream job," as I often heard from passengers, whenever I shared a turtle shell or a beaver pelt. "Sure is," I often replied, smiling, or trying to smile, then adding, "I also teach at the university in town. Environmental studies." A part-time position, I rarely admitted. Not much pay.

I continue to sift through these feelings about who I was and who I've become—a man always wandering, searching, struggling. Always expecting the worst. Always restless. I think of Pitman and Shaw creeks, whether I was born there decades ago, if not in the valley itself, then in those circumstances. I remember Dad's drawl, his bloodshot eyes and cigarette smoke, how the odor gave way to creek air, cool and damp. Was I stepping away from him, or toward the water? I can't tell anymore. Maybe I never could.

Then I think of Paula, a park ranger I met out west. Dad would've been proud of my marriage, how I've lived my life. He used to call me Indiana Jones, after the movies starring Harrison Ford, and in his trailer he kept a photo of me hiking in the mountains. In it my eyes are bright. My face is tan. I'm grinning. I had mailed it with a Christmas card, crossing thousands of miles.

SUBJECT: ADVICE FOR TREE HUGGERS

Dear ENV 303 students,

A long email. Please take time to read it.

For starters, remember that for Thursday's class, 3/28, we're hiking in Greens Coulee Park in Onalaska. Meet at the bus in front of the PAC. We'll depart at 12:40 and return by 2:05. You can leave your bag on the bus, though you might want to carry a water bottle. Dress for a mile-long ramble up a slushy trail. We'll need to hustle to reach the viewpoint. Plan to sweat!

As for today's class, thanks for an engaging discussion about the personal side of sustainability. I figured we'd run out of time, but I appreciate your openness, your passion, your willingness to imagine your life in the years ahead. We tend to dream outward from our academic interests, our "major," and how our schooling will lead to a career. The career we expect. Then to a house, marriage, kids, whatever the order. And you talked about your twenties—a time for adventure, you said, to live it up. Are other cultures like that, other college students, or is this unique to Americans? We claim the future. We expect!

That said, I hope that by discussing some of the *unexpected* situations I have faced over the years, you get a sense of the terrain ahead. This journey is not a straight line. It's not predictable. There's no guarantee of anything, though you often reach your goals but not in the way you mapped out. There's something called a circumstance. Then another. And another. You guessed it: real life.

By that I mean you have to make choices based on any number of variables at a particular time. Personal variables. And the process is seldom simple, or easy. You do the best you can, and sometimes you feel regret. Or another way of saying it: Making a choice is often not the hardest part. Living with what you have chosen—that's what's tough. That's the work. That's the day-to-day journey. It influences how you view your past, how you feel in the present, and how you might act in the future. Like I said, real life.

So how does any of this relate to ENV 303: Issues in Environmental Sustainability?

Sustainability *is* personal. No matter what anyone says about devoting their career to the environment, or devoting their lifestyle, we're always forced to address basic needs. *Your* needs: your health and wealth, your job, your family, your map of expectations. And you can scheme all you want about using less fossil fuel, or eating organically, or supporting local businesses, but human nature always prevails. Self-preservation prevails.

That may be the biggest challenge each of us faces as a tree hugger: to commit personally and consistently to living with conservation as a priority. It's so easy to let it slip. Our circumstances invite that slip. Real life does.

Imagine how hard it is to get other people to care about the environment the way you do right now. If this is a career path you'd like to pursue, start figuring out how to relate to people, to get inside their heads, their hearts, and to learn what really matters to them. Because there, always there, you'll find everything we discussed today. Dreams and expectations. Needs, circumstances, the self. If you're not listening to those concerns, people won't listen to you.

To sum it all up, here's my advice, though keep in mind I'm still trying to follow it myself:

- Save money and watch your debt. It's difficult to reach your goals if you're stressed out all the time, especially due to finances. A marriage, let alone an environmental ethic, will crumble because of such stress. Start saving now. Learn how to invest. Imagine if your career turns sour, and how you'll survive when it does. Think in terms of generating wealth over time, not just having a job. The latter will change more than you know. When it happens, lick your wounds. Get over it. Begin again.

- Follow your heart and bust your ass, though don't expect fairness. Real life is not fair. But don't take personally the actions of others—your boss, your coworkers, even your friends. Most people are doing the best they can, given the circumstances defining their lives. Of course, there are plenty of jerks out there, so be wary. Protect yourself. Protect what matters most to you.

- What matters most? Love, including loving yourself. Figure out what you love, who you love, and why. Hold on to them. Grow together.

- And last but not least, go outside. You'll never regret a hike. If there's anything I would prioritize for a sustainable life, a life devoted to the environment, to caring for it, it's time out of doors. Out of walls. Out of ceilings. It's time to get muddy, slushy, sweaty. You will not care for what you do not know. Start now. Start knowing it.

That's what we'll do on Thursday. A trail can teach you what I cannot!

—Jeff

Jeff,

It's safe to say you just slid into first place for my favorite teacher of all time. Thanks for an awesome class yesterday and a fantastic email. I'll take your advice to heart.

—Kaitlyn

RED

July 24, 2016
Pipe Spring National Monument, Moccasin, AZ

Unloading the groceries last night beneath the luminescent spiral of the Milky Way, its horizon-wide arc fading into skyglow—suburbs, casinos, three-thousand-room hotels—I heard Red kicking his trough, begging. I've come to know that sound, that rhythm, a slow cadence in the high-desert darkness, every time my headlights swing through the corral and as I step from my car door to the hatchback. *Boom. Boom.* I've come to know it, to cherish it. I know now a retired Grand Canyon mule, though lanky and rickety and three decades old, thinks he's in charge of this place. He is, actually. At least he's in charge of my date this morning. In Carhartts and work gloves and old uniform boots, Paula and I will shovel manure and walk the boys.

We've lived at Pipe Spring for nearly two years now. Federal property, forty acres, a postage stamp of sagebrush and juniper, apples, peaches, plums. It's surrounded by the 120,000-acre reservation of the Kaibab Band of Paiutes. Their ancestral homeland. Their origin stories. And as the monument's website explains, generations of "American

Indians, Mormon ranchers, plants, animals, and many others have depended on the life-giving water," just as we now depend on it to drink, bathe, wash our clothes. We depend on decades-old snowmelt trickling through sandstone.

Come to think of it, until Paula applied to be the interpretive manager of this site, a position requiring year-round residence in this small, dust-covered house—a position she took to get back into the National Park Service after four years with Fish and Wildlife—I hadn't known about Pipe Spring. Hadn't even heard of it. Hadn't lived with rattlesnakes in the wood pile either. Hadn't watched a black widow up close, chased a jackrabbit, or hiked a trail from the back door, up a cliff face, and then set my hand in a dinosaur's track—a theropod, according to my field guide. A carnivore. It walked this ground 180 million years ago.

This is all my way of saying that life along the Arizona Strip has surprised us. The affection we feel, the welcome. Yet we cannot stay. We know this. The remoteness and isolation are unsustainable. This summer, I'm home only on my days off from Zion, about a two-hour drive given Springdale's tourist crowds; stop for groceries and it's three. And in those hours, as I skirt the geology of the Grand Staircase—the Pink Cliffs, Gray, White, Vermilion—my mind veers to what-ifs: What if I never have a year-round job again? What if the stock market tanks? What if my back pain worsens and I can't commute? This life is beautiful but exhausting.

None of that matters this morning. Red's waiting. The horse, Rowdy. The steers, the chickens, the ducks. Our cupboard's full. We've got a date.

Still, I'm thinking about our Kaibab neighbors, how they exist here, how they endure. *It is not remote*, they might say. *This place is our center. We are of it.* I realize I haven't felt that way in years, and I fear never feeling it again. I should close this journal, that's for sure. I should head outside to the orchard. From there it's a few steps to the mule.

"Apples," Paula says. "He loves apples."

A LITTLE LEAGUE
ALL HER OWN

Men are what their mothers made them.

—RALPH WALDO EMERSON, *The Conduct of Life*

By the summer of 1978, a few weeks before the fourth grade, all I knew about football had come from playing in neighborhood pickup games. Touchdowns, offsides, "smear the queer." Grass stains and bruises. Plus what I'd learned from television, when gladiators battled in colossal stadiums, the screen crackling at a fever pitch. Roger Staubach on the Dallas Cowboys. Terry Bradshaw on the Pittsburgh Steelers. Real men, real tough.

I liked Jack Youngblood too. A scary name, I thought, fun to yell. He sacked quarterbacks, which kind of killed them, and played on the Rams, the LA Rams. "Rams! Rams!" Also fun to yell. "Rams! Rams!" I'd raise my arms, swearing. And I'd imagine the yellow horns painted on Youngblood's helmet. Swirling horns. Horns! Blood!

Football was a war game at nine years old. Medieval combat. Clashing clans. I hadn't a clue, I know now, but at least I'd figured out bravado. We named ourselves after our favorite pros and threw wobbly spirals with a plastic ball. Its fake threads and rock-hard tips hurt your fingers, your palms, your chest. You'd hide the hurt, had to. You'd catch, run, get tackled. And no matter what, everyone had to keep the ball from skidding to the back of the lawn where septic pipes drained with ooze. It was slippery there. It reeked. "No one tackles in the shit," an older boy would say. "Don't run into the shit. Got it?" I understood: Stay inbounds. Don't be a pussy. Take a hit.

I remember Johnny Marley and Paul Graham, Fritz and Karl Fentz, and sometimes the Fentzes' cousin, Keith Ramsey, a city-bred, thick-necked bully who tackled like a juvenile delinquent. Elbows in your face. Kidney punches. He once gave me a wedgie so mean, so thorough and textbook perfect, he tore my underwear and bloodied my back as his fingernails gouged beneath my waistband. Moments later, back on my feet, angry, crying, I felt the fabric flutter behind me as I ran and juked and spun.

I hated Keith Ramsey. He smeared and smeared. He was Jack Youngblood. He was the horns.

Despite its punishment, football had plans for me. As August neared, Johnny's dad handed my mother a flyer calling for kids to register for a full-contact Little League. "Sounds good for you," Mom said. "How about we sign you up?" I agreed to make her happy—I needed to toughen up. She was getting tougher too. My father was no longer around.

The autumn games would take place on Saturday mornings in Fortville, Indiana, a blue-collar town in the corn and bean fields northeast of Indianapolis. The practices would start at 5:00 p.m. beside my school two miles from home, in a vacant lot with sagging goalposts and dusty, pebbled turf. I was the only boy my grade in the neighborhood; none of the others would be on my team. Carpooling wasn't an option, and Alan, who was in high school, had yet to get his license. But my grandmother lived next door to us and worked the early shift at Western Electric, so she agreed to drop me off if Mom could pick me up. Mom worked days in the city at a Red Lobster restaurant, about thirty minutes from my practice in rural Hancock County. She could make it by six thirty if she drove straight there from work. My job was to make a snack for myself before getting into Grandma's car. A latchkey kid's promise, necessary for years. I ate bowls of Cheerios, PB&Js, and countless Little Debbies.

For me to play, of course, we needed to purchase equipment, but the task was far more difficult than Mom and I had expected. We'd assumed that finding gear would be back-to-school easy, as if outfitting a kid for football was like picking out pens and paper. Shortly before my first practice, we roamed from one store to another, holding the list Mom had written down from a raspy voice on the phone. It took two or three nights of searching—the shelves were picked over. Each stop was a lesson on laces, stiff snaps, and stretchy straps. We sized up shoulder pads and black cleats, mesh jerseys and tight pants, then a nylon belt stumped us as I cinched it around my waist. Its tail dangled below my knees, and I felt minuscule, fragile. "Don't worry, ma'am," the salesman said. "Just cut and singe the end."

Little by little, our shopping bags filled with everything but a helmet. I must've tried on a dozen or more, each size and model too tight. My skull was huge and oblong—a watermelon, elongated. My forehead ached with red marks, my ears from failed attempts. Mom asked a store manager to check the size and shape of my head, so he circled a tape measure through my hair, grumbling under his breath. He double-checked the number, raised his eyebrows, and checked again.

"No wonder," he said. "Your son needs a seven and a half. I'll have to special-order it and custom-fit the pads."

Mom stood beside me in the mirror in a blue dress with a shiny name tag, a uniform she wore to work every day in a little league all her own. She was beautiful with long black hair, red lipstick, and painted nails. Whenever she smiled, I looked "on the bright side," a phrase she still likes to say.

Yet when she agreed with that man, my shoulders sank with embarrassment. I realized what lay ahead, at least I thought I did. Practice would start in a couple of days, full of boys I barely knew, and I'd walk on the field without a helmet, a pussy on the very first play.

Sure enough, when Grandma dropped me off to start my Little League career, I stepped from her car wearing full pads without my special-order helmet. I couldn't participate in "bull in the ring"—a tackling drill that kind of killed kids—so the raspy voice told me to run laps as others gathered for scrimmaging. And I remember learning blocking assignments with somebody's dad, an assistant coach. He pulled my jersey by the collar and barked orders, pointing his finger. "That's your man, Muse! Stay low, drive your legs!" Then he dragged me away from the line so that my teammates could pummel each other.

I hated the crybaby treatment, hated sticking out. I wanted to be like the other boys, their faces obscured by cages. I could see the white athletic tape stretching across their helmets, and read the fat black letters spelling their tough last names: GORDON, HAYES, McKEEMAN. Would they be like Keith Ramsey? I stood on the sideline, fretting, shrinking, chewing and chewing on my mouthpiece.

When the store manager called Mom, we made plans to go straight from practice. I changed in the backseat, relieved to drive to Indianapolis. The store's entrance jangled when we opened the door, and I smelled leather—the smell of sports— an aroma that thrilled and intimidated me, a reaction I have to this day. And I recall when the manager emerged from a back room, box in hand. I was seconds away from fitting in. My new helmet would set everything straight.

But my stomach collapsed. An implosion. Humiliation! The man lifted the helmet, massive and gleaming, nothing like Youngblood's horns. Instead, it was bulbous like an insect's head, as goofy as a morning cartoon. Its light gray face mask had two spindly crossbars with a vertical, clipped-on T. It was twice the size of what my teammates wore. "No!" I whined. "That's for wimps." If I showed up wearing *that* helmet, the jokes alone would kick my ass.

Here's the thing: every Little Leaguer knows this. Your reputation is at stake, your identity. When you lean into your stance, knuckles in the turf, looking like you belong is half the battle. Feeling it, well, that takes years.

The store manager lifted the helmet, crowning me the king of misfits. He pulled it down, then took it off, exchanging and tweaking the pads.

"You're fine," Mom said, smiling in the mirror as she tightened my uneven chinstrap. Her son had chicken legs and a chicken-hearted torso, topped off with a prize-winning pumpkin. I realize now I wanted to quit then, and would have had Mom allowed it. I realize, too, that she couldn't quit and my playing football was for both of us.

In my fifties, I still think about that helmet whenever I try on ball caps. Labels often read "One size fits all," but seldom does that mean it'll fit *my* head. Each time a hat disappoints me, I remember those self-conscious days. I recall that little boy, fretting and shrinking, wanting to quit and walk away. Yet somehow I made it through Little League, then playing in high school and college. I can't pinpoint how I did it, only that Mom was there, always there, always cheering. And sometimes my grandmother came along. If not, she'd support me back home. But there wasn't a game—a single game in any season—that my father showed up to sit in the stands.

At nineteen, I began to figure this out. I began to understand that what troubled me wasn't the size of my helmet but the insecurity inside it, the fear, an unnerving secret. It came to me one evening after practice during my sophomore year at DePauw University, a prestigious school, picturesque, a haven for wealthy midwesterners. I'd squeaked in thanks to good grades and financial aid and because I'd attended the Tigers' football camp for teenagers. At camp, I'd met DePauw's head coach, Nick Morouzis, a wiry man with a rousing voice. Not raspy. Rousing! He loved to yell, a fun yell, especially when you were sweating, aching, arguing with self-talk. "You gotta want it, baby!" Coach Nick would holler, never swearing, never letting up. And I did, I wanted it, wanted it bad. I became a Tiger.

Coach Nick wore thick glasses and smiled a lot, seeming to dole out constant praise. I even took his on-the-field critiques as tough love from a spirited mentor. It was easy to trust Coach Nick, who treated everyone like he belonged. But that evening after practice, when I needed to confide in him, I didn't feel comfortable at all.

I walked toward Coach Nick as he stood outside the locker room. I was still in my pads, carrying my helmet. And I waited as he talked with one of my teammates who was bigger, faster, stronger. I watched as a little man counseled a giant boy, thinking about all the years I'd kept up. By then I'd lifted literally tons of weights. I'd memorized playbooks. I looked the part.

"Coach," I asked, when he glanced my way, "can I talk to you a minute?"

"Sure, son," he said. I wanted privacy. He could tell.

I needed to ask for his permission to miss a practice the following week, but the request was unusually personal and I wasn't sure how he'd respond. My father was in jail at the time. Drunk driving. Dad *was* a drunk. But a union lawyer had arranged for his release to a treatment center near Kokomo. My brother and I needed to visit him; reconciliation was part of the plea. Coach Nick could see my embarrassment. He'd met my mother. Only Mom.

"I don't want anyone to know," I said, looking down at the concrete. Dozens of cleats scraped by. Other boys. Other men.

Whatever the potential of a latchkey kid, it seemed like a half-kept promise. I felt like an imposter standing there. I'd hidden the hurt, the secret.

I looked up when Coach Nick patted my shoulder pads. "It's not your fault," he said. "But you have to make the best of it, Jeff. That's all we can do sometimes."

In that moment I didn't know what to think. I'd gotten permission, but what else? I thanked him and stepped toward the steam, toward the doctors and lawyers of tomorrow. The room was filled with echoes—showers, jokes, banging metal. I opened my locker, hung up my helmet, and slipped in my sweat-soaked pads.

A year later I would recall that conversation, the night after our game against Wittenberg. The Tigers had won 14–10, and my block on a long punt return had helped. After the game, I drove to Indianapolis, where my brother was getting married in his church. I wore a black tuxedo like the older groomsmen, all gathering near the altar with Alan. But I stayed in the lobby, waiting. Headlights trickled past, then vanished. I didn't know if Dad had a license, but he'd said he'd be there, that he wouldn't miss it. Later, when I called him, he said he'd gotten lost, that a buddy had been driving and they'd gotten drunk. I listened to his slurring, the round-and-round apology, making the best of it, I guess. I couldn't quit.

Last night, facing a mirror, I looked at my middle-aged torso. I can't bench-press 340 pounds anymore, but my bodyweight is still 180, the same as my playing days at DePauw. My six-pack of yore is a proud four. Once a linebacker, always a linebacker.

I also looked up Keith Ramsey online, discovering his obituary from 2016. He passed away at only fifty years old; no cause of death was given, only condolences. As I read the comments of the grieving, I was reminded that each of us leaves behind a legacy in the memory of others, a collective memory that the dead will never know. In Keith's case, the obituary said he was a general manager for MCL Cafeterias throughout Indiana, and that in his younger years, he had wrestled and played football. He was a Lawrence North Wildcat, class of 1985. He "enjoyed camping and was an avid fisherman and outdoorsman." And there he was, shredding my underwear, swearing, terrorizing my memory, yet he'd also been "a member of the jazz singing group" in high school.

I got my ass kicked by a choir boy? I'm not sure I can accept that.

What I mean is, Keith Ramsey will forever be one of the meanest, orneriest kids on the planet, and I need him there, in that memory. Perhaps it's an unfair, one-dimensional memory, but I need it to make sense of my insecurity, my fear, and to overcome them.

It is much the same with my father. I understand now that his absence was a foe, or a line of scrimmage demanding that I stand my ground. Mom fought there in her own way against Dad's drinking, his excuses, his choices. It's possible, as well, that my father did try to attend my ball games, much as he tried to attend my brother's wedding. It's possible that he knew—and Mom may have said as much—it was best for him to stay away, giving my brother and me stability, giving *her* stability. We may have all been chicken hearted, all scared, all needing to suck it up. Family life can be brutal. Clans break.

These are difficult questions to tackle. I haven't even figured out the questions. For instance, what was it like for my mother when I started playing football less than a year after her divorce at thirty-two? She had not only begun raising two boys on her own but also climbing the long ladder out of poverty. How did she have any time for my practices and games?

In the late 1970s, the US divorce rate was reaching its historic peak. More than half of all married couples were splitting up, many with young children. As a child, I knew nothing of such statistics, nothing of anyone's hardship or insecurity. Instead, I felt only that my family was different from the others living along East 38th Street. Paul Graham and the Fentz boys had two parents in their houses, older couples, long married, as I recall. And Johnny Marley's dad had always lived alone—the elder bachelor who made everyone laugh. Yet when he handed my mother that flyer, did he understand the toll a divorce takes? I saw his son only occasionally due to his own custody agreement, but John Sr. also knew my father through Chrysler. Was he keeping tabs on us, for Dad?

Even so, how could anyone have known what my mother was going through at the time? Who was that woman standing beside me in the mirror, tugging on my chinstrap, making the best of it? Indeed, during my first football season, Mom would sometimes arrive before practice had ended. She'd walk toward the field as my teammates and I ran wind sprints, though stop short of all the dads on the sideline. Instead, she'd sit on the parking lot curb, slip off her heels, and lie back on the concrete. Between sprints, I'd watch her, my hands on my knees, till the whistle blew and I had to run again.

Recently, I asked her about those August evenings, if she was exhausted from her job or single parenthood. What she remembers, she said, is the warm sidewalk. "How good it felt. How we'd be all right."

HOOSIER

During that winter Japhy had hitchhiked up to his home-country in the Northwest, up through Portland in snow, farther up to the blue ice glacier country, finally northern Washington on the farm of a friend in the Nooksack Valley, a week in a berrypicker's splitshake cabin, and a few climbs around. The names like "Nooksack" and "Mount Baker National Forest" excited in my mind a beautiful crystal vision of snow and ice and pines in the Far North of my childhood dreams.

—JACK KEROUAC, *The Dharma Bums*

The little slacker! On Memorial Day in 2019, my oldest nephew, who was twenty-one, skinny, antsy, and fresh out of college, group-texted a selfie video from Albert Mountain. He was standing beside a fire lookout in western North Carolina, at mile one hundred of the Appalachian Trail, the AT. I'm talking about Henry, Henry Alan Muse, who gets his last name from my dad, an alcoholic he never met, and his middle name from my brother, who's my elder by seven years. As for Henry, that's his alone—an original in our family—and for more than two decades now, whenever I talk *to* him, it's the closest I can get to what a parent might feel. Or maybe just an uncle, from a Latin word for "little grandfather."

Which brings up an important point: this isn't an essay about an unresolved desire to have children, not on my part, not on my wife's. We made that decision years ago when I married an older woman, a federal park ranger to whom I've committed and recommitted as we've moved around the country. Paula never wanted kids, and given my bouts of gloom and the instability of transience, not to mention we both believe the planet needs fewer humans, I'm good with little grandfathering. And frankly, seeing what happened to my brother's family—divorce, financial hardship, the bitterness that endures—I'd just as soon be childless because my luck would be no different.

So let's start here, with Albert Mountain. Pull up a satellite map of the Tar Heel State and zoom in where Tennessee, Georgia, and South Carolina form its westernmost point in the Nantahala National Forest. See that deep-green patch packed with amphibians and fungi and flowering plants? It's a hideout, a refuge, where countless species rode out the ice ages and threw a kind of orgy. It's a montane Shangri-La, a mecca for biodiversity. I don't know if Henry grasped that when he hiked to 5,200 feet, but he was there, and I wasn't, so when I watched his twenty-second video, I leapt a little in my skin. I leapt because I was excited, and because I was jealous. "Get a job," my brother likely grumbled. Me? I'm still wondering.

Or let me put it this way: Albert Mountain is a six-hour drive from Charleston, where Paula and I have lived for nearly four years, and where I write this essay in May 2020. I'm on lockdown, we all are, sheltering in place due to the COVID-19 pandemic. That's right, stuck in Chucktown, America's "Best Small City" according to *Condé Nast Traveler*. But in truth, I'm bored here, or rather, out of place. To paraphrase the poet Theodore Roethke, I have failed to live up to the geography. Because *Condé Nast* is right: Charleston is special. Scenic, sultry, seductive, but also stone-cold sobering, with block after block of oak-wrapped architecture largely built by slaves. And besides its melting-pot history, from English, Scottish, and Spanish to French, Barbadian, and Native American, all overshadowed by African cultures that formed the Gullah Geechee, there's Charleston's food, outstanding food—shrimp and grits, rice and beans, okra, yams, collard greens, fish this, pork that, biscuits and gravy and . . . you get my point. This town tantalizes. It's both horrific and intoxicating.

But also flat. Absurdly flat. It's the flattest, steamiest, most closed-in place I've ever lived. And that's saying a lot because like my nephew, I'm a midwesterner. We both grew up in central Indiana, where industrial farmland and sprawling suburbs either numb you into complacency, at least in terms of the environment, or they inspire you to escape to higher, wilder terrain. What I mean is, when Henry texted that wobbly video, wobbly because he was breathing hard and mountain buzzed, jacked up on eye candy, layer after layer of outcrops and meadowy balds and blue ridges—and good lord, think of the streams, the whitewater, the sound of gravity—pride and envy flooded my gut, and what felt like an emotional sugar high that quickly crashed into angst.

"Right on!" I typed, the good uncle. "2,100 to go."

"You can only come from one place," wrote Bob Cowser Jr., one of my MFA professors, "and it sticks with you, good and bad." As I've been writing my own book, my first real stab at a book, I've realized again and again I'm a Hoosier. I grew up in cornfields, in flat, featureless country, where my parents built a brick one story, then divorced and got poorer. I will always be from there. I will always be *of* there. It sticks with me, as Cowser said, good and bad.

What's a Hoosier? No one knows for sure. The name was forged through folklore in the early 1800s, when Indiana marked the woodsy frontier north of the Ohio River. Some historians attribute the moniker to a man named Samuel Hoosier, a contractor who hired burly types to build canals near Louisville, Kentucky. "Hoosier's men" became Hoosiers. That's that, end of story.

Others prefer the more colorful tale of pioneers yelling a query through locked-tight cabin doors. Who's rustling in the darkness, looming, unseen? Imagine wondering friend or foe while grabbing your rifle and powder, the same tools you use to put food on the table—squirrel, rabbit, turkey. "Who's 'ere?" you might holler. Would the Shawnee answer back?

And don't forget the brawls, the tavern brawls, in river towns with mixed company. A man walks in and steps on something, something squishy, something bloody. "Whose ear?" he asks nonchalantly, curious but not surprised. Indiana boys are present. Bump into one, expect a knife fight.

There are innumerable stories like this. Not all are silly, but all seem to reach for a mythos, an archetype, a Hoosier ideal that's even portrayed in the state seal: a stout Lincoln-like character taking an axe to an old-growth hardwood; a bison, woolly and wild-eyed, jumping over a felled tree, presumably to some place uncut; and perhaps silliest of all, the sun setting over small mountains. This has always baffled me. Indiana is not mountainous, not by any stretch of the imagination. Its highest point, Hoosier Hill, at 1,257 feet, is actually a miles-wide pile of glacial debris near the Ohio state line, rising about thirty feet above the surrounding farmland. Even southern Indiana's rolling woods and hollows have a vertical relief of only three hundred feet. The ski area Paoli Peaks, for instance, trundles along with artificial snow.

What highlands, then, are we talking about? Historian Jacob Dunn, in 1919, interpreted the state seal: "It is not a 'setting sun,' but a sun rising on a new commonwealth, west of the mountains, by which, at that time, was always meant to be the Allegheny Mountains." Huh? In Pennsylvania, three hundred miles east of Indiana? "The woodman represented civilization subduing the wilderness; and the buffalo, going west, represented the primitive life retiring in that direction before the advance of civilization."

"Retiring," as in relaxing? How quaint. Skedaddle west.

I have no reason to disagree with Dunn, but I'm still annoyed. I'm annoyed because Indiana—its state seal, its mythology—is a con job. It's a con job like so many of the neighborhoods I've known since youth, all named for what they wish they had, or what they actually did have before the bulldozers and construction crews showed up. You know the type: Deer Crossing, Fox Hollow, Woodhaven, "a land where every place is like no place in particular," as James Kuntsler wrote in *The Geography of Nowhere*, a book I read the final summer I lived with my mother in Fishers, Indiana. Talk about suburbia. Talk about a son bringing his mom down. Every day in Fishers, in the 1990s, was a bloodletting. Another forest felled for a housing development. Another creek straightened. Another so-called park designated not for nature restored but for soccer fields. For ball diamonds. For retention ponds with shorelines that weed whackers kept clearing of cattails.

But critters can retire, no? They can skedaddle?

"Be positive," Mom said. "You're so mouthy." And so I tried. I tried to be positive because those neighborhoods meant progress, a progress my single mother could claim as her own. But I'm not disparaging those locations, or her. I'm lamenting them. I'm lamenting them because I know Henry and his siblings and too many kids in too many American neighborhoods are also getting conned. But they don't even get the benefit of seeing the trees before the bulldozers arrive, before the braggadocio of economic growth kicks in. Their homes went up in cornfields, or what had been cornfields in the good ol' days. My days. My myths.

I wouldn't dare say half of this to Henry. This toxic cynicism. And I didn't when I picked him up at Sams Gap at the North Carolina–Tennessee line, about ten days after his text. I'd driven northwest from Charleston on I-26, rising from the heat and humidity of the Lowcountry's coastal plain, through the Piedmont, into the lush, leafy hills surrounding Asheville. And then I climbed higher—into drizzling gray clouds, cool air, and layer after layer of outcrops and meadowy balds and blue ridges. As I pulled into a parking spot near the trailhead, I saw Henry ambling toward me, unhurried, hiking poles in hand. He'd just stepped off the Appalachian Trail, mile marker 315.3.

"You stink!" I said, hugging him. My arms reached around his backpack, which was small, lightweight. He was walking twenty miles a day.

"Yep," he said, smiling. "Hungry too. Got any snacks?"

I lifted the tailgate of my Subaru so he could sit down and take off his shoes. "Thru-hikers," he called them. The soles were ungluing. They reeked of sweat and sogginess, of dark nights in a stuffy tent. He'd traveled through Great Smoky Mountains National Park without much of a view. "It rained the whole stretch."

"Here, wear these," I said, pulling out my Chaco sandals. Then came the bag of pretzels. I knew he'd be craving salt.

And for the next two days, my lanky nephew and I hunkered down in Asheville, staying in a hotel as more downpours drenched the region. Among the tasks on our list was celebrating his twenty-second birthday, plus a trip to Recreational Equipment, Inc., REI, to consider new shoes. A laundromat, a food run, then a med-check—his ears were plugged with wax. In our room he unpacked his grimy gear, not much, really, far less than I've carried on short backcountry trips, but everything he needed. Indeed, there was little I could teach him; he had mastered going light. But as our room filled with the sprawl of his airing-out tent, his rainwear, and the assorted contents of stuff sacks, the stink enveloped everything, especially from those thru-hikers. "Try this," I said, grabbing a *USA Today*. I crumpled newsprint inside his shoes, sucking up the moisture.

I had wondered how Henry would respond to civilization—a hotel room with television. He didn't care for the remote, instead using the Wi-Fi and his headphones. He was content to dry out, it seemed, and perhaps to let his guard down. He'd mentioned lightning strikes in the high country, the trail shrouded in mist. I thought about my own stint on the AT, up in Maine, during my first round of grad school. The path turned into a streambed as storms pummeled the route.

To be honest, I questioned whether Henry and I had become different from one another, if we'd grown apart. It seemed that way at first. Whereas I was filled with impatience—to talk, to listen, to sightsee in Asheville—he was mellow. He was on trail time. Henry was moving through life very deliberately in those hours, and just as he relished the clarity of organizing his backpack with precision, obsessive precision, readying for a long walk, he also embraced a day off. And it was obvious he was off. I'd brought a change of clothes for him to wear while doing laundry the first night, yet he kept wearing them for two days straight, through sleep, through restaurants, through shopping at REI. He poked around the hotel room wearing only my boxers. I looked at the sprout of hair on his chest, his scraggly whiskers, his fiercely wavy black mop, and realized he'd grown up.

And when we did talk, he made it clear that he was aware of paying off his school loans, of the need to get a job and figure out his future. His degree was in communications. "Anything goes," he said. But I could also see how proud he was, how happy, happy to be in the moment, to live moment by moment. Not only the camp chores and adapting to the weather, but also the steady pull of mile after mile down the trail. Or *up* the trail. AT hikers climb northward from Georgia to Maine, and Henry had more than three months to go.

"What's your trail name?" I asked, remembering the age-old tradition. People who attempt the entire distance give each other nicknames.

"Glide," he answered. "Everybody thinks I'm fast. They say I make it look easy." I thought about the tension my brother used to talk about—getting Henry up, getting his homework done, getting him out the door.

"Perfect," I said, admiring my flesh and blood. I felt like his little grandfather, glad to pal around. I snapped a photo of the hotel room and texted it to Alan. I included my mother, who replied thumbs-up.

Yes, we Hoosiers love a good story, especially those we tell about ourselves. Case in point, my forebears named the state for the very thing they couldn't abide yet wanted to emulate: the Indians. "The primitive life," as Dunn put it.

Is that good? Is that bad? Does it make Indiana any different from anywhere else? I don't know. What I do know is that my nephew, like me, has that itch, that restlessness that comes with realizing you identify with the bison more than the woodman, with looking west more than east. I can see it in his video, still on my phone. The boy's hooked. Hooked on hiking, on exploring, on lighting out.

Only days before he summited Albert Mountain, Henry had graduated from Ball State University in Muncie, not far from Hoosier Hill, and his text carried me back to my own youth, my first summer out of DePauw when I worked at a YMCA camp on the Flat Rock River, southeast of Indianapolis. I wore hiking boots and cargo shorts and tied a red bandanna around my head, whatever I thought people were supposed to wear as environmental educators, a job that chose me as much as I chose it. And whenever I broke away from the kids, I buried my nose in books like John Muir's *My First Summer in the Sierra* and Barry Lopez's *Arctic Dreams*. I pictured myself on a trail in some faraway unknown, and began making plans. I began working up the courage to believe the story I was telling myself—a story I'm still telling myself, you can bet. And I bet it's the same story Henry is starting to tell himself: "The mountains are calling and I must go."

John Muir wrote that, but you get my point. This myth making, this restlessness, this primordial itch lies inside you, and you don't know if it awakens with a book, a felled suburban woods, or your first hard look in the mirror as part of a broken family, and you can only scratch that itch—itchy as all get-out—on the go. You start figuring out *who* you are and *where* you are are practically one and the same, and you're in your twenties, feeling that first hint of numbness, and you know the time has come: either jump the log or not.

Then again, isn't that what it means to be a Hoosier—to light out, to forge a new life on the edge of the unknown? No wonder my forebears were proud. No wonder their stories, their aspirations. Whether I understood it or not, I carried on their tradition when I moved west my first time at Henry's age, jobless, hungry, literally hungry. I landed about as far as I could go in Washington state. To me, a cornfield kid, the Pacific Northwest *was* the frontier: a storm-lashed coast, snowy summits, and sinewy, salmon-fat streams racing through conifers and Indian reservations. I didn't know anybody—the people themselves were a wilderness. And for the better part of three decades, with a little time spent elsewhere, I gave the West some of my best seasons, got married, even got wealthier. Yet here I am now, stuck in Chucktown, on lockdown. Have I forgotten my heritage? Am I still a Hoosier? Will I ever light out again?

In early 2020, before the pandemic hit, Henry called me from I-40 as he and his girlfriend, Jordyn, departed Petrified Forest National Park in northeastern Arizona, adjacent to the Navajo Nation. They'd been hiking in scablands all day, after camping in a moonlit wash. As Jordyn drove, Henry sat in the passenger seat, taking in a kaleidoscopic sunset. They were headed west to Flagstaff to sleep in a Walmart parking lot.

"See any ponderosas yet?" I asked.

"No, it's pretty barren," he said. "Looks flat out there."

"You're climbing," I said. "Expect juniper, piñon, then ponderosa pine. By the time you get to Walmart, you'll be at seven thousand feet. Bundle up."

I reminded him that Aunt Paula went to Northern Arizona University. "She calls the town Flag. Lots of skiers and mountain bikers." I talked about turning south on I-17, dropping off the Mogollon Rim to Phoenix, to the warmth of the Sonoran Desert, to saguaro and ocotillo. "They might be blooming already. It's beautiful. Check it out." But Henry and Jordyn, off work for only a week, were headed north to Utah, first to Zion, with thousands of others most likely. "When I rangered there," I offered, "I learned one thing about the crowds: if you don't want to wait in line for an hour, get through the gate by 8:00 a.m."

"We've got reservations," he said, "in Watchman Campground. That should make our mornings easier. I've got it all planned out."

I wonder if Henry appreciates how much I enjoy our chats. We talk about geography, about the character and culture of places. What we don't talk about is what burdens this Hoosier these days, what makes me, in my fifties, more conflicted than he is—more conflicted than most young travelers, including myself at twenty-two. Back then I knew only wanderlust and treated boredom like failure. Now it feels like a privilege, especially for White men. I never thought twice about such freedom, even when I was poor. I could sleep in my car most anywhere and never be bothered. I realize, too, that national parks and America's public lands have come at a cost to Indigenous people. Even John Muir knew that. His evangelism caused exclusion. Exclusion on the heels of genocide.

Yet my burdens are more self-centered. As much as I've embraced itinerancy due to my wife's career, though also because Henry's elders have long busted up families, I've also suffered the consequences—jobs cut short, friends left behind, relationships severed by restlessness. Fact is, when you begin thinking that who you are depends on where you are, a problem can emerge: complaining becomes self-destruction because no one likes a complainer. No mother. No wife. No place, for that matter. You're either planting roots or not.

But I continue to struggle. I struggle to reconcile reality with romance, with naïve notions of exploring a place and possibly calling it home. Take Zion National Park, that sandstone Shangri-La. When I worked there as a seasonal ranger, I'd patrol Riverside Walk, which leads to the world-famous Narrows, where hundreds of people would consume my attention as they trudged through the Virgin River. The dozens of hand-stacked rock formations I dismantled on each patrol revealed a larger story of countless and constant impacts: humans feeding wildlife, humans damaging a rare habitat, humans leaving behind soiled clothes and bodily waste and trash, not to mention the loss of solitude, the loss of "the primitive life."

My frontier in Zion was everyone else's, but what must the Southern Paiute feel? *Mukuntuweap*, "straight canyon," is sacred.

I oftentimes wish I didn't know these things, or think about them, or question them. And I don't want Henry to, not yet at least. I want him to have what I had, if only his sense of discovery and wild places to discover—indeed, a privilege. At the same time, I realize he's walking into a world far more crowded and threatened than the one I knew thirty years ago, and that, thanks to the internet, he may know more about it than I did at his age. He researches. He plans. I also recognize that his home ground—my home ground—isn't as soulless as I've made it out to be. Fishers, Indiana, may be suburbia, but it's riven with streams, streams defiantly winding through woods, slim woods but woods nonetheless. There's even a new "agripark," a thirty-acre patch of public land cultivated as a community farm. Now that's positive. That's worth bragging about.

But what *is* lost these days? Not just what wildness, but what ways of stepping out into that world, the unknown world, looming, unseen? Aren't we all bearing a cost as the sacred becomes mundane? What is lighting out to new territory when you can simply look it up online?

And so it was, when the rains finally let up in Asheville, that I drove my Hoosier nephew the half hour back up to Sams Gap, mile marker 315.3 on the AT. His backpack was carefully organized. His shoes, the same shoes, still reeked. And with hiking poles in one hand, a scone from breakfast in the other, Henry stepped through a small gate to begin ascending the thin, rocky path toward Maine. I watched him round the corner into a woods—my little grandson, happy, I think—then I turned back toward my car for the long drive home, downhill all the way to Charleston.

WE BROTHERS
OF THIS HOUSE

February 11, 2021
McLeod Plantation Historic Site, James Island, SC

Five days a week, wearing khaki pants and a dark blue uniform shirt, I climb the stairs inside the McLeod House, the center of a former cotton plantation that enslaved up to one hundred African Americans at the outbreak of the Civil War. Built in 1854, it's essentially a three-story lookout, situated on high ground and designed to surveil a forced labor camp. The house has thirty-three windows, eight fireplaces, echoey twelve-foot ceilings, and rich, reddish planks of longleaf pine flooring, old growth, tightly grained. Without question, enslaved craftsmen helped build it, as with most of antebellum Charleston. I marvel at their expertise, not to mention their stolen labor.

My work computer, perched atop a standing desk, sits in what had been the bedroom of William Wallace McLeod, a White man born in 1820 on nearby Edisto Island. He was an ardent secessionist, an occasional politician, and the vice president of a local committee advocating to reopen the transatlantic slave trade. In 1861, near the height of his wealth, McLeod also presided over the agricultural and police society for the St. Andrews Parish, which included his home. That means he oversaw the slave patrol. And I suppose, given the depth of his racism, it wasn't a big leap for him to take up arms to defend it. He died a Confederate soldier, of dysentery, near the war's end.

But it's another man in uniform, Black, nineteen years old, who captures my imagination—and with whom I feel kinship. On April 2, 1865, he signed his name on a plaster wall on the third floor above my office: "George Smothers, 55th Mass. Co. G."

Who was this US soldier, why was he in the McLeod House, and why did he take *his* leap, which is almost unfathomable? Nearly 156 years after his visit, I've teamed up with a coworker to research Smothers's life, and the lives of other men and women known to have been here, in order to write social media posts for Black History Month. The experience has been gripping, and surprisingly personal. Smothers's journey reads like a novel, a tale of survival, duty, and doggedness through circumstances beyond his control.

George W. Smothers was born on April 15, 1845, in Franklin County, Virginia, and died from stomach cancer on February 16, 1911, in Arkansas City, Kansas. As his obituary stated:

His family moved to Indiana when he was three years old, lived there until he was eighteen years old, when he enlisted in the 55th Infantry, Mass., serving two years and six months in the war. In 1871 he came to Kansas and filed on his farm 2 1/2 miles west of town, on which he lived until three years ago when he moved to the city.

We've yet to uncover how young George's family "moved" from slaveholding Virginia to Indiana, a free state. Did they escape on the Underground Railroad, crossing fold after fold of the Appalachian Mountains and then the Ohio River? Or were they already free people of color, as Franklin County is known to have had? Laney Allison, whose partner is Scott Preston, a great-great-grandson of Smothers, emailed these clues, which seem to indicate that young George was separated from his family until around the time of his enlistment: "He traveled from Virginia to Indiana as a child and lived with families, the Todd and later the Woods [race unknown]. In 1863 he united with his mother, Evaline Jennings-Smothers and older brother, Charles and older sister, Frances in Indiana."

On January 1, 1863, President Lincoln's Emancipation Proclamation allowed Black men to begin serving in the United States military. Smothers, then living in Farmland, Indiana, traveled to Readville, Massachusetts, to enlist. Joining Company G of the Mass. 55th Volunteer Infantry, the sister Black regiment of the storied Mass. 54th, he would be among the more than two hundred thousand African

Americans in the US Army and Navy by the end of the Civil War. Before departing the Charleston area, the Mass. 55th joined the New York 54th, a White regiment, in occupying McLeod Plantation from mid-March to April 4, 1865. Two days before he left, Private Smothers ventured up the same stairs I climb each week, but rose two flights higher, entering what had been the quarters for enslaved domestic servants prior to the war. On the chimney wall, in large, swooping cursive, he penned his autograph, adding the line "James Island, April 2."

Did Smothers leave his signature after sleeping in that very spot? Or did he ascend the stairs out of curiosity, investigating a house that had been commandeered by Confederate officers? And why had he—free, literate, likely educated in a school founded by White Quakers and the Black community in the vicinity of Farmland—volunteered to put himself in harm's way? I can't say that I know, that I truly know. Smothers and I may share a Hoosier heritage, but our circumstances are profoundly different.

Nonetheless, Laney Allison offered more clues:

[George] returned to Indiana after his honorable discharge from the Civil War in 1865 where he remained until he relocated to Kansas to homestead. It was said he and a friend walked the last 125 miles to stake his claim and farm his land. He lived the remainder of his days in Arkansas City as a pillar of the community, a founding member of Saint James AME Church, a member of the colored Mason's Grand Lodge, appointed to the Southwestern Soldier's Association, and well respected by all, whether white or black.

He was remarkable; that much is clear. Yet this leads to more questions—the job of a historical interpreter. My colleagues and I dig and dig. Census records, land claims, pension files.

For example, did Private Smothers, in his dark blue uniform, realize that during the time he was emancipating enslaved African Americans, fellow US Army soldiers were helping to decimate Indigenous cultures in the West? "Bleeding Kansas," where Smothers would settle after the war, had been admitted to the Union in 1861, after unprecedented violence between proslavery "Border Ruffians" and antislavery "Free-Staters." And Oklahoma, named for the Choctaw words meaning "red people," would not become a state until 1907. When Smothers helped found Arkansas City along the Kansas-Oklahoma border, he would live on the edge of "Indian Territory," lands set aside by the US government for tens of thousands of aboriginal people forcibly removed from their homes. Smothers's farm itself, located in the fertile bottomlands of the Arkansas River, had been Wichita country—someone else's country. Did he understand his part in this battle of colors and creeds and ways of life?

I doubt it. I doubt it because I myself don't understand. I didn't, growing up, and I struggle to do so now. I'm a middle-aged park ranger, an environmental educator reinventing a wayward career. It occurs to me that as a boy in rural Indiana, Smothers no sooner could've expected to liberate an East Coast plantation and one day push out Plains Indians than I could've imagined my own work inside a White supremacist's master bedroom, pecking out Facebook posts. And certainly McLeod never planned to die of diarrhea and dehydration, much less see two wives and four children die, and then wither in an unknown grave. We may all be men of destiny, we brothers of this house, but none of us has a damn clue.

The best we can do, I'm realizing, is move toward the horizon with an open mind and an open heart, as Smothers seems to have done. As an anonymous remembrance in his local newspaper said, "he was kindly and unostentatiously, to all with whom he came in contact, a helper and a friend." A good man. A fair man. I hope I'm following in his footsteps. Up the stairs I go.

DEAR PARK RANGER

In one of my favorite photos of ours, from September 2006, after most of the high country's snow had melted yet before the storms of autumn, you're hiking up a steep, trailless slope in North Cascades National Park. Whatcom Peak rises in the background, pyramid shaped, glacier flanked, as distant wildfires haze the sky to a pale white in afternoon warmth. We're near the international border, not far from home, in the footsteps of Henry Custer, the cartographer who surveyed the Northwest Boundary in 1859. You're smiling. Your heart is full. Your expression is pure contentment—with me, with our surroundings, with the pack on your back, with the sweat. Moisture glistens on your cheeks and neck after several miles of uphill exertion. You're wearing sunglasses and a pink ball cap. Your black ponytail is threaded with gray. And on your right knee you're wearing a neoprene sleeve, a reminder that you're forty-one—not old, of course, but no longer a kid, no longer a young wilderness ranger. It's day four, maybe five, of our ten-day trip in the park. We're on our way to Bear Lake, a blue jewel beneath Mount Redoubt.

One thing I love about you, and I can see this in the photograph, is that you don't give up easily on anything. On that mountain you're resting in a talus field, wearing a backpack that towers above your head. What you may not know is that I weighed your pack before we left home for the trailhead. I wanted to see if it was heavier than mine, and it was, which irritated me. I wanted to be a man—*the* man, stronger—so I took part of your load when you were in the garage or out watering the flowers. I stuffed the tent fly into my pack, took a fuel bottle, the trowel. I reorganized some of the food, did it clandestinely, had to. You would've resisted, shouldering it all just to prove a point. I admire that, I do. What I don't like is my insecurity.

Looking back, I realize this trip was similar to our first date in April 1999, a warm afternoon, a Saturday, when we hiked toward Fourth of July Pass, postholing through snowdrifts. I fell for you that day—fell hard, trying to keep up.

Do you remember the knee-deep snow, my sopping-wet boots, and our aching, early season thighs, how you churned through drift after drift, trying to find the buried trail? I didn't care that we'd lost the route; I was watching you, your backside. You wore formfitting tights beneath Patagonia shorts. You were svelte. Such long legs. I stepped in your steps in my sagging cotton socks and a T-shirt I'd worn while coaching football. "Cotton's got no business in the backcountry," you said, and I laughed, pleased with your swagger. But as long as we kept moving, I'd be fine, plenty warm, and I knew I'd keep looking at your ass. I'd never hiked behind a park ranger before, let alone through snowdrifts.

I fell hard, fell fast, postholing.

Then again, this is when I fell, a single moment twenty-two years ago: I was focusing on the gaiters covering your boots, which were army green like your work uniform. Although it was your day off, you'd been acting like a ranger, clearing limbs from the trail when we'd come upon it. As we took a water break, our skin steaming, ball caps off, you pulled your hair into a ponytail—lustrous, like raven feathers. And in that moment as you paused for a drink, I wanted to reach for you, to say how beautiful you were, how rooted. But you startled me with a shout. "Look, glacier lilies!"

You grabbed my hand, both hands, pulling us toward a sunny ledge. "See them?" you asked. "My favorite."

We lowered to the ground, our butts in the air, to examine a tiny trio. Green leaves cupped yellow petals like delicate half-open palms, fingers stretching skyward. I had never seen a wildflower in the snow before, or heard that one could generate its own heat. But there it was, poking through ice, thawing a circle an inch or two wide.

You plucked a petal gently, tore it in half, and handed me a piece. "Try it," you said. "Tastes like sweet corn."

I placed the creamy sliver on my tongue, chewing slowly, timidly at first. You were right: a taste from a summertime garden, something I'd known countless times back in Indiana.

"Reminds me of home," I said, though in that moment, I wanted nothing of cornfields and flat farmland, and certainly nothing of football. I wanted the mountains. I wanted to hike. I wanted to find every wildflower. I wanted you.

Later that spring, at the end of work on a Friday, damp and cloudy, you asked me to join you for the memorial service for Scott Croll, held at the Park Service compound in Marblemount. I think it was my first time in the Wilderness Information Center—"the wilderness office," you called it. I saw the group photos on the wall, season after season of the backcountry staff, and your face in many of them, your long black hair, your contentment. On the counter were pies, fresh bread, and covered dishes—the makings of a potluck. I shook hands with twenty people who had gathered to honor Scott, his longtime friends and former coworkers, men and women who'd moved on from seasonal employment to take so-called real jobs. Most had been "noka" wilderness rangers at one time or another, now working as educators and scientists, administrators and cops, many with advanced degrees. Some had babies in their arms. They asked about my work for North Cascades Institute, about the environmental learning center I'd been hired to help design in the park. They asked if I liked to climb, to hike, if I'd been up Big Beaver or Thunder Creek. I listened mostly. I was in love—with you, with them, with the story of Scott.

During the service you squeezed my hand as you cried. It scared me. It scared me to see everyone crying as they shared reflections about Scott's adventurous, contemplative life, his years as a climbing ranger and on Ross Lake, how he had liked to sail, to roam, to write. Someone explained his recent death in Alaska, where his plane had disappeared over Glacier Bay. Foul weather, hail perhaps. No wreckage found. No body.

That evening or the next, or another near-solstice weekend when the daylight stretched on and on—the half-light, the sun-behind-the-mountains light, with the trill of varied thrushes in the woods, the ever-present echo of Diobsud Creek plunging with snowmelt, the smell of fir needles and thimbleberry and spring-warmed soil—we sat on the back porch of the old City Light house you rented from Ralph Dexter. Or rather it was the front porch, the small wooden stoop facing the horse pasture, the fruit trees, and a white-topped ridge rising a vertical mile. You talked about your life in the park since 1985, starting as a student intern, then working as a seasonal employee and eventually becoming a "permanent." You talked about your summers in a lookout cabin on the six-thousand-foot spine of Copper Ridge. You talked about patrolling trails and campsites in the shadow of Mount Baker, Shuksan, Redoubt. And then you showed me a worn, softcover book, *On the Loose*, by two young brothers, Terry and Renny Russell.

"For years it's been like my Bible," you said, thumbing through its pages, pulling out pressed leaves, little notes you'd written, and your own sketches and photographs. The Russells had created the book back in the sixties, celebrating wildlands in the American West. You read this passage aloud, saying that "it explains why I do what I do":

> One of the best paying professions is getting ahold of pieces of country in your mind, learning their smell and their moods, sorting out the pieces of a view, deciding what grows there and why, how many steps that hill will take, where this creek winds and where it meets the other one below, what elevation timberline is now, whether you can walk this reef at low tide or have to climb around, which contour lines on a map mean better cliffs or mountains. This is the best kind of ownership and the most permanent.

I think a lot about that old City Light house. I think about the Russell brothers. I think about "getting ahold of pieces of country" in my mind, trying to feel ownership of those places, trying to belong. More than two decades after our first hike together—after moving from Washington to Wisconsin, to Arizona, to South Carolina, and now helping you apply to another park out west because, as Wallace Stegner said, the West is "the geography of hope"—what I know for sure is that I belong to you. And you to me. The way we belong to each other has been a profession unto itself. A calling. It's how we survive, and sometimes thrive. To love and to cherish, to protect, isn't that what a park ranger does?

Part of what we must protect is our story. The bad with the good.

I know now that rangering is more than shouldering a heavy pack or postholing through snowdrifts. More than pie and fresh bread at potlucks. More than front-porch kisses that go on and on like the half-light of summer along the forty-ninth parallel. It's also bad ankles, bad knees, and bad backs. Mosquitoes, ticks, exhaustion. I know that the season is too short, the pay too little. I know that marriage counseling has helped us, and that depression has not only been my burden, but also yours. I know that rangering is a discrimination lawsuit you're not supposed to talk about, nondisclosure agreements being what they are. But fuck that. It's been nine years since the settlement, and you can now say whatever you want about how you were treated by those who wore the same uniform as you. Who still wear it. You can say how you lost your community, your identity, your ownership.

But you don't have to. It's *your* story to tell, not mine. You can say or do whatever you want, wherever we are, and I will support you. You can be whoever you want to be. And know this, dear park ranger, beloved wife: I'm right behind you, beside you, step by step, and like you, like glacier lilies, I don't give up easily on anything. I have faith the sun will be there once we burn through the snow.

CODA

Lying on the lawn tonight, the valley top in alpenglow, I watched a hummingbird skim the bee balm as dragonflies patrolled in zigzags. The upriver breeze, summer-warm, steady, cascaded through us—our lungs, our cells, our spirits. Everything swayed with the field grass, the alders, the cottonwoods, as Paula circled round the garden, in its second season like our house. She named the best growers and those needing help—water, weeding, a trellis. She pulled spinach for dinner, a few garlic tops. Snap peas for Sonny and Pablo. "Excuse me," she said to a toad in the lettuce, the wind weaving through her hair, mountainward.

July 15, 2007

Martin Road, Rockport, WA

ACKNOWLEDGMENTS

On the title page of *The Paradise of Bombs*, published early in his career, Scott Russell Sanders signed his name and wrote: "To Jeff—the book where I learned in public how to write essays." I am indebted to Scott, who has been both mentor and friend, father figure and muse. Not only did he provide a letter of recommendation to help me get into a graduate program in creative writing, but he and his wife, Ruth, have also welcomed Paula and me into their home about an hour from where I grew up. And it was Scott's example—his writing about family, place, and finding one's way in the world—that encouraged me to learn "in public" too. I write essays because Scott does. Had I, in my twenties, not picked up *The Paradise of Bombs* and *Secrets of the Universe* and *Staying Put*, I wouldn't have understood that the essay, especially the personal essay, is more than a paragraph someone submits with a college application. For me, essays are compass bearings and unplanned meanderings, mountain trails and river trips—ways not just to make sense of my life, but to live it. They are my maps, unbound by destination.

I thank the publications in which many of these essays, or earlier versions of them, appeared: "I Remember the Dogs," previously titled "The Big Bang," in *Poydras Review*; "An Ark of the Heart," previously titled "Ground Truthing," in *Flycatcher*; "Trailblazers," previously titled "Manly Labor," in

Soundings Review; "Deer's Ears," previously titled "Anima," in *Poecology*; "The Moon, the River, a Best Friend," previously titled "Skagit River, Washington," in *Orion's* The Place Where You Live and *The Good Men Project*; "From Fire Lookouts to Slave Cabins," as several paragraphs in "Busted Beer Cans and Baby Culture," in *High Country News*; "SAR Talk" in *The Common*; "A Rucksack Rumination," as several paragraphs in "Sauk Mountain, North Cascades, Washington," in *EarthLines*, as well as in its current form in *The Wayfarer*; "One Mighty Yank," as several paragraphs in "Patience and Pluck," in *La Crosse Magazine*; "Waiting for Rain," previously titled "Pitman Creek," in *Ascent* and *The Good Men Project*; "A Little League All Her Own," previously titled "Tough Love," in *Stymie: A Journal of Sport, Games, and Literature*; and "Red," previously titled "Making my peace with the desert—and a mule," in the *Christian Science Monitor*.

Special thanks to Shawn Halifax, Jake Lees, Leslie Crislip Nielsen, Ted O'Connell, and Ginny Taylor for reading early versions of this manuscript and offering essential feedback. Thanks, too, to Jill Christman, Bob Cowser Jr., Sonya Huber, and the faculty, staff, and students in the MFA program at Ashland University, where several of these essays were born. Likewise, I appreciate the help of Joe Wilkins and students in the *Orion* Online Environmental Writers' Workshop. Christina Roth, an independent editor, was also indispensable in sharpening sentences to clarify my voice. Likewise, without

Les Browning and the team at Homebound Publications, my final manuscript would not have been printed.

Thanks, as well, to my family, the living and the long gone, and to friends and others who appear in these pages (some of their names have been changed for privacy). In particular, my love for my mother is beyond any expression of gratitude.

Lastly, my humblest, most heartfelt thanks go to Ranger Paula. This book would not exist without her willingness to share our lives, our journey. May we grow old together, holding hands. May we plant gardens, watch birds, and keep hiking.

ABOUT THE AUTHOR

Raised amid cornfields, Jeff Darren Muse is a fatherless, childless Hoosier who wouldn't and couldn't stay put. With master's degrees in science and creative writing, he has worked throughout the United States as an environmental educator, historical interpreter, and park ranger, occasionally publishing essays. Exploring nature, culture, family life, and his own highs and lows, Muse's writing has appeared in *Ascent, The Common, High Country News,* and *River Teeth,* among others. Today, he and his wife, also a park ranger, live at the foot of the Sangre de Cristo Mountains in Santa Fe, New Mexico.

WAYFARER

BASED IN THE BERKSHIRE MOUNTAINS, MASS.

The Wayfarer Magazine. Since 2012, *The Wayfarer* has been offering literature, interviews, and art with the intention to inspires our readers, enrich their lives, and highlight the power for agency and change-making that each individual holds. By our definition, a wayfarer is one whose inner-compass is ever-oriented to truth, wisdom, healing, and beauty in their own wandering. *The Wayfarer's* mission as a publication is to foster a community of contemplative voices and provide readers with resources and perspectives that support them in their own journey.

Wayfarer Books is our newest imprint! After nearly 10 years in print, *The Wayfarer Magazine* is branching out from our magazine to become a full-fledged publishing house offering full-length works of eco-literature!

Wayfarer Farm & Retreat is our latest endeavor, springing up in the Berkshire Mountains of Massachusetts. Set to open to the public in 2025, the 15-acre retreat will offer workshops, farm-to-table dinners, off-grid retreat cabins, and artist residencies.

HOMEBOUND
PUBLICATIONS

Since 2011 We are an award-winning independent publisher striving to ensure that the mainstream is not the only stream. More than a company, we are a community of writers and readers exploring the larger questions we face as a global village. It is our intention to preserve contemplative storytelling. We publish full-length introspective works of creative non-fiction, literary fiction, and poetry.

Look for Our Imprints Little Bound Books, Owl House Books,
The Wayfarer Magazine, Wayfarer Books & Navigator Graphics

WWW.HOMEBOUNDPUBLICATIONS.COM

Printed in the USA
CPSIA information can be obtained
at www.ICGtesting.com
CBHW031624251123
2113CB00004B/10